God's Love, Your Life

A New Look at Discipleship, Christian Faith and Love

Henry Thomas Hamblin

Hamblin Vision Publishing

Copyright

© Copyright 2025 Hamblin Vision Publishing - all rights reserved.

The content contained within this book may not be reproduced, duplicated or transmitted without direct written permission from the author or the publisher.

Under no circumstances will any blame or legal responsibility be held against the publisher, or author, for any damages, reparation, or monetary loss due to the information contained within this book, either directly or indirectly.

Legal Notice:

This book is copyright protected. It is only for personal use. You cannot amend, distribute, sell, use, quote or paraphrase any part, or the content within this book, without the consent of the author or publisher.

Disclaimer Notice:

Please note the information contained within this document is for educational and entertainment purposes only. All effort has been executed to present accurate, up to date, reliable, complete information. No warranties of any kind are declared or implied. Readers acknowledge that the author is not engaged in the rendering of legal, financial, medical or professional advice. The content within this book has been derived from various sources. Please consult a licensed professional before attempting any techniques outlined in this book.

By reading this document, the reader agrees that under no circumstances is the author responsible for any losses, direct or indirect, that are incurred as a result of the use of the information contained within this document, including, but not limited to, errors, omissions, or inaccuracies.

Contents

Concise Biography of Henry Thomas Hamblin	VII
Preface	XX
1. The Unfolding Life	1
2. A New Commandment	9
3. The Love Which Passeth Knowledge	16
4. Living the Harmonious Life	26
5. The Life Victorious	34
6. The More Abundant Life	43
7. Living the Universal Life	52
8. The Problem of Evil	56
9. Reason and Intuition	63
10. Divine Plenty	72
11. Supply Consciousness	82
12. Health	93
13. Wholeness	101
14. Prayer	110

15. Blessing and Forgiveness	120
16. Steadfastness of Spirit	130
17. Our Father Who Art in Heaven	136
18. Hallowed Be Thy Name	142
19. Thy Kingdom Come	150
20. Thy Will Be Done	155
21. Give Us This Day Our Daily Bread	159
22. Forgive Us Our Trespasses	162
23. Lead Us Not Into Temptation	166
Also by Henry Thomas Hamblin	172

Concise Biography of Henry Thomas Hamblin

BY JOHN DELAFIELD, HAMBLIN'S
GRANDSON

Who was Henry Thomas Hamblin?

Henry Thomas Hamblin was a spiritual teacher and writer based in Sussex, England, whose message and vision were straightforward and pragmatic. He believed that the spiritual life and the practical, everyday life were inseparable. His teachings centred around the power of thought and the importance of meditation to draw on the inner power, wisdom and love that we all have deep within us. Hamblin referred to this as 'the Secret Place of the Most High' in the days before meditation was widely practised in the West.

Hamblin was colloquially known as HTH, and later 'the Saint of Sussex'. Whilst his teachings leaned towards esoteric Christianity, his philosophy was truly universal, embracing the truths of all faiths. The emphasis of his message is on finding the power of spirituality within us all, in the context of our everyday lives, rather than religion. As a young man, he reacted against the dogma of his strict, religious upbringing, and believed that religion often divided people, while spirituality united people. His teachings came from a place of pure empathy and compassion for humankind.

Henry Thomas Hamblin worked right up to the end of his life in 1958 and left a legacy that continues to this day, its voice as much needed now as it ever was.

A Wayward Child

Henry Thomas Hamblin was born in 1873 in Walworth, South East London, of Kentish parents, and was the second of two sons. His father was very religious, and his grandfather a minister of the Baptist Church. His mother, although of diminutive size, was reportedly 'great of soul' and ruled the family with benevolent autocracy. The family was poor, very poor, like all those living around them in that district of London in the late Victorian era, and, despite their hard work, the only education that could be afforded for Henry was an elementary one. He followed this with a course in technology, which proved to be of inestimable value to a youth who was considered by his parents and teachers to be wayward.

"Unstable as water; thou shall not excel," his mother reproached him regularly. No doubt she intended it to shame her son into a regime of self-improvement, in keeping with child-rearing practices of the time, but it was hardly confidence-inspiring! "Slacker!" was the repeated insult from his elder brother. Wiser, more objective, heads might have paused for long enough to recognise a certain potential in the young boy who, at the age of nine, could attempt the writing of a school newspaper. He had also established himself as something of an elocutionist. Writing and speaking would both prove valuable skills in later life.

His adolescent years gave little indication of an error in the family verdict. 'Henry the wayward' moved from one poorly-paid post to another, idled in between dead-end jobs, succumbed to bouts of ill-health, and, before he had reached the age of eighteen, had displayed more than the usual 'adolescent failings', according to his autobiography, *The Story of My Life*. From a modern perspective, all these Victorian euphemisms point to Hamblin being something of a 'bad lad', an impression added to by his own heavy hints that he had been no stranger to drinking and carousing. He suffered terribly from pangs of regret following his periods of over-indulgence, so that 'Henry the sinner' became 'Henry the saint' – until the next time. His pronounced rebellious streak landed him in hot water more than once. He constantly pushed against the boundaries of the fire-and-brimstone brand of Christianity in which he had been raised, which he felt to be unbearably restrictive. Reading about his struggles with authority as a young man somehow makes the rather aloof spiritual writer he became more accessible and endearing; it's hard not to warm to someone who so openly confesses their own faults and shortcomings, especially in the tightly buttoned-up era in which he lived. He was inspired by books, many of which fired his worldly ambition and prompted his spiritual imagination.

What his parents and educators overlooked was that Hamblin was a young man with huge aspiration, flushed with a youthful zest for life, and inspired by a worthy ambition to rise above the rut of his circumstances. Although he pushed against his father's dogmatic and punitive style of practising religion, at heart, he was deeply religious. A person's early environment, education, and adolescent behaviour can often determine the course of their life. Youthful indulgences of one sort or another are inevitable. Hamblin's studies of the New Testament, which revealed that selfishness and hypocrisy, rather than indulgence, received greater condemnation by Jesus, would have been very much in his consciousness.

A Successful Businessman

There is no doubt that Hamblin had an enquiring mind, and this, coupled with a desire for scientific accuracy, enabled him to achieve success in his later endeavours in business. In this, despite his lack of education, he was bolstered by boundless faith and courage, which, coupled with a shrewd business sense, ensured that he succeeded beyond all expectation. In 1898, having taught himself ophthalmics at night, he qualified as an optician and set up his first successful business as an optician, Theodore Hamblin (now Dolland and Aitchison), frequented by royalty, the rich and the famous.

Hamblin was a natural entrepreneur and a born risk-taker. By this time, he was also a family man. He married Eva Elizabeth in 1902, and they went on to have two sons and a daughter. He enjoyed acquiring several businesses, all with insufficient capital, and relying on credit and goodwill. He took more pleasure in the thrill of the challenge than in the promise of monetary gain. Far from being downcast in the face of numerous setbacks, he thrived on negotiating obstacles which appeared insurmountable. As soon as the business was established and running smoothly, however, rather than being satisfied with financial security and the ability to provide for his family, Hamblin's interest started to wane. He felt a loss of the initial drive and motivation, his physical and mental health began to decline... until the next big idea came along and away he would charge again, all fired up and raring to go.

Throughout all his wild days of youth and high-risk business ventures, Hamblin felt a great tug towards discovering a deeper meaning to life, beyond that of the daily struggle to make ends meet. Propelled by his discontent, he became a driven seeker after truth. In his quest, he met other prominent thinkers of the time and formed lasting friendships.

As his business success grew, so did a gnawing sense of depression. It was as if there was something inside him that had not yet found a voice. Around this time, he discovered the New Thought movement and began to read their publications. Hamblin realised then that none of his worldly success had made him happy. He felt that a move from London to the coast would be beneficial.

Shortly afterwards came the outbreak of the First World War, and Hamblin went off to serve his country, leaving his business in the care of others, almost with a sense of gleeful relief, strange though it sounds. But it was the sudden and unexpected death of his younger son at the age of ten, in 1918, that brought him to rock bottom and he began to question everything.

A Very Practical Mystic

Hamblin was not a genius, and millions of other people have made good in the world with even less promising assets. But it was in the second half of his life, when Hamblin turned away from creating highly successful business enterprises to focus instead on the spiritual realm, that his unique combination of the pragmatic and the profoundly spiritual shone forth. He has sometimes been described as a very practical mystic.

Hamblin began writing in the 1920s. The words seemed to flow from him. He found that writing clarified his thoughts. One of his first books written in this new phase of his career was *Within You Is The Power*, which was to sell over 200,000 copies. Other books soon followed. Hamblin believed that there is a source of abundance which, when contacted, could change a person's entire life. As long as people blamed their external circumstances for any misfortune, they were stuck in the 'victim role'; but if they moved in harmony with their inner source, their life could be full of abundance and harmony.

Soon after this, Hamblin set up a magazine called *The Science of Thought Review*, based on the principles of Applied Right Thinking. He wasn't discouraged by the fact that he had no experience of editing or publishing. His experience had taught him that if the mind worked in harmony with the Divine, then everything you needed flowed towards you. Anyone with any business sense at all knew that to set up a magazine with a first print run of 10,000 copies would be a risky thing to do. But Hamblin was not risk averse, to put it mildly! He wanted to put what he believed into practice. The only magazine of its kind in the 1920s, it soon gained a worldwide readership. Among his friends and contemporaries that were to contribute to the magazine were Joel Goldsmith, Henry Victor Morgan, Graham Ikin, Clare Cameron and Derek Neville, all of them prolific and successful writers. Apart from his international subscribers, Hamblin had close ties to comparative spiritual thinkers in many other countries, especially in the U.S.

Although he had been brought up in a strictly religious family, he hadn't found any of the answers he sought in the Church. He realised that, rather than following any creed or dogma, which didn't work for him anyway, he had to look within himself. He found contact with 'Presence' and realised it held the key to the peace he was seeking. All the time, his search was leading him nearer to discovering the way his thoughts affected his performance and outlook.

During the General Strike of 1926, the Great Depression of 1929-32, and again in years after the end of the Second World

War, many homeless, unemployed wayfarers came to the Hamblin household seeking relief and shelter. Henry and Elizabeth provided them with a simple meal, new boots and clothing, and money for the road. Hamblin was a man who applied his spiritual principles to his everyday life. Practical Mysticism was Hamblin's life's work. He helped people, in practical ways, to become less fearful, happier, and more successful in their lives. To this end, he wrote books like *The Antidote to Worry*. However, later in life he realised that whilst these books genuinely helped people, they were largely concerned with the personality. He then wished to go a step further and become more fully a truly 'practical mystic', so he wrote a spiritual course of 26 lessons, each with a definite theme presented in a systematic way. This was designed to move beyond the constraints of personality so that the soul could breathe the pure air of Spirit. What was needed, he felt, was 'a total surrender of ourselves to the Divine.' The course is available as the book *The Way of the Practical Mystic*.

The Power of Thought

Hamblin was at the forefront of the New Thought movement which was gaining pace in the early 20th century. He discovered that 'new thought' was, in fact, ancient wisdom, based upon the truth that has always existed since before time began. All great souls give voice to that timeless truth in a myriad of different ways. Hamblin urges us to "Think in harmony with the Universal

Mind." In other words, he underlines the fact that truth is and cannot be changed depending upon our mood or our whim.

Hamblin realised that we need not only a positive frame of mind but an applied way of thinking - Right Thinking, as he termed it. What did he mean by that? Essentially, he defines Right Thinking as:

- Thinking from the Divine standpoint.

- Controlling the thoughts so they do not go off on negative tangents away from the Divine Truth, which is always positive.

- Replacing negative thoughts with positive thoughts.

- Living in the consciousness that all is well; and as an adjunct to this, remembering that perfection exists as a reality now, and to think in the consciousness of that knowledge.

- Meditation or prayer is the highest form of Right Thinking.

- Ultimately, however, the aim is to get beyond thought, 'to enter ultimate truth'.

He said, "When we cease thinking, we glide out on the ocean of God's Peace. Thought brings us to the foot of the mountain after which we have to proceed by intuition."

> *Health, Wealth and Happiness. Isn't this something we all want, either for ourselves or for those dear to us? And yet, how many of us are struggling to reach or hold such a goal for a sustained period of time?'*

Hamblin's teachings explain how we can achieve all of these things, not by hard work and striving but by a simple change of thought. *Within You is the Power* is one of his simple but profound statements, and the title of one of his books.

Hamblin was a prolific author and had many thousands of followers studying and benefiting from his teachings and courses until his death in 1958. The simple principles contained in those teachings are as relevant today as they were when he was alive, and can still help us to achieve health, prosperity and happiness if we apply them conscientiously.

He died in 1958 in Chichester Hospital. The Hamblin Trust exists to this day to propagate the legacy of his work.

The Relevance of his Teachings Today

Hamblin was, essentially, a Christian mystic, yet his ideas about the simplicity and clarity of presence seem incredibly contemporary. He believed that the source of all wisdom is within us and all around us, and that this is the fundamental reality; there is no separation, and we are all one. His message and advice to all who read his work is that it is for everyone and is in harmony with the aspiration of all good people throughout time. Hamblin believed that there can be no finite creed of an infinite faith. Moreover, he suggests that, when creeds appear, true faith can be constrained.

He cautioned that if you seek God in prayer, the corollary is that you must have faith in Him. He often stressed that no prayer goes unanswered, and, although you may not get the answer requested, your prayer will be answered in some form. God is around us and within us, and this is the fundamental reality. He made it clear that, although human organisations come and go, God's laws are eternal, and that God is the quintessence of love, wisdom, and harmony. He expresses the clear view that "Blessed are they who believe and yet have not seen". The knowledge that God is born within us is fundamental to our understanding, and only by the loss of self can God be found. At the point a person surrenders his or her 'self' to God, it is then that a re-birth takes place and one's real life in God begins.

Some may question this view and ask: "What is this but the core teachings of the many brands of Christianity?" In response, Hamblin's view was that modern Christianity is a heterogeneous compound of the teachings of Jesus interwoven with historic pagan-based doubts and fears, litanies, supplications and more, all of which are closely guarded by a priestly hierarchy. These were strong views, and Hamblin does not disparage those who found them uncomfortable, as he says that churches are necessary and helpful for those who are succoured by them. Hamblin had a lifelong rebellious streak where authority was concerned, and this included the strictures of the Church. Hamblin would sometimes say that the Truth of the message of Jesus was so often wrapped up in dogma and creed that its purity and simplicity were obscured.

In his teaching, he states that first comes purity of intention, reminding his readers that one cannot serve God and Mammon. Either you trust God completely or you hedge your bets by having worldly alliances and a healthy bank balance. He maintains that trying to achieve both will impair spiritual development. Secondly, an individual's dedication to following God's path will require great patience, perseverance, faith and courage; but in following this path, the individual will develop forbearance and good will. He adds that other life experiences will follow naturally and lead to a developing compassion, which will enable the individual to radiate the love of God.

Where should we place Hamblin in the long line of mystics, seekers and finders? Perhaps it is rather impertinent to pose the question some 65 years after his death, but it is surely relevant to consider this point as, by any measure, he was an extraordinary person.

Remember that he was born into a life of poverty and obscurity but, despite a very limited education, by superhuman efforts of his imagination, he rose to wealth and secured an esteemed position in life, while all the time being aware of another "self" within him, a spiritual self. Dramatically, in the middle part of his life, he surrendered his material successes to follow his wider calling as a disciple of God. In this later life, he did not subscribe to any specific creed or form of religion. He was no haloed saint in the traditional sense, but he would have said, "What I have done, or rather what has been done through me, can be done by any person in the world according to their gifts and personal faith".

The essence of this teaching is that the latent power of God lies within everyone.

John Delafield is the grandson of Henry Thomas Hamblin and a retired RAF pilot. The majority of his childhood was spent living with his grandparents, Henry Thomas and Elizabeth Eva Hamblin.

Preface

Prayer is the soul's sincere desire,
Uttered or unexpressed,
The motion of a hidden fire
That trembles in the breast.

~ James Montgomery

The timely message of this little book should make a wide and far-reaching appeal. It is a word very greatly necessary in these present days of disquietude, when amid uncertainty and questioning, and quickened, perhaps, by the increasing pressure of events, we are more heedful to the deeper note of truth. The superficial philosophy which by process or thought would win a surface good, to the deprivation of the spirit, all too satisfied with the gourds and trinkets, the vanities, the glitter and tinsel, the passing show as if such were the real: it is all swept aside, and shown for what it is, and in its place, what is indeed worth striving for, depicted; the reality, in very truth, out of which all that is worthwhile has its origin, and without which all that comes is but a 'vexation of spirit'. "Seek ye first the Kingdom of Heaven, and its righteousness, and all shall be added unto you." First things must be first, if other things are to follow in their sequential order. If we minister there, we will be surely ministered unto. In this central loyalty we will find our joy-note, and it will ring through our whole experience.

The theme of the book is a progression from the valley to the heights. We are led to the Hill of the Lord, which may be ascended only by those who are "of clean hands and pure heart". And the ascent is humankind's achievement of the mystic consciousness. Appropriately, it ends with a fine study of prayer itself, prayer which Montgomery described as "the soul's sincere desire, uttered or unexpressed", for it becomes ultimately God's desire in us. These chapters will be found particularly helpful, especially to those who come to them simply, desirous of the practical aid which assuredly they will find. We are glad to see the Lord's Prayer so wisely and helpfully analysed. Here we come to the altitude, and there is a glow upon the words. But fine as the inspiration is, the writer sees more than he can express. There is a point where words fail.

The message rings through all the pages, "If with all your hearts ye truly seek Him, ye shall ever surely find Him. Trust in Him." The author presses from the unreal to the real, finding there the solace of his heart, the answer to his aspiration, the rich satisfaction to his desire. Further, it is not of ourselves we can do these things; we must let God do it, putting the reins in His Hands.

Very warmly do I give a "God-speed" to this uplifting little book, trusting that it may achieve the wide influence that it deserves.

Richard Whitwell

>He prayeth best who loveth best,
>All things both great and small,
>For the dear God that loveth us,
>He made and loveth all.
>
>>Paradise Lost ~ John Milton

Chapter One

The Unfolding Life

> Is not prayer a study of truth – a sally of the soul into the unfound infinite? No man ever prayed heartily without learning something; but when a faithful thinker, resolute to detach every object from personal relations, and see it in the light of thought, shall, at the same time, kindle science with the fire of the holiest affections, then will God go forth anew into the creation.
>
> Ralph Waldo Emerson

It is in the everyday life, in "the mud and scum of things",[1] that we find those experiences which are most valuable in our spiritual unfoldment. When once we have entered the path, everything in life, no matter how mundane or prosaic it may be, is an

---

1. From Ralph Waldo Emerson's poem "Each and All"

experience specially suited to our spiritual needs. That is to say, if it be taken in the right way, it helps us along the path, introducing us to a deeper and richer knowledge of God.

Every difficulty or disappointment is a trial of our faith; every unpleasant incident a test of our goodwill or universal love. There is a lesson in everything, and we are wise if we learn it.

Whatever we do, if rightly regarded, may prove a stepping-stone in the way of life. There is a lesson to be learned from each experience that will help us in our upward climb.

God needs His witnesses in every employment, to ennoble the same. The more we co-operate with life's experiences, the happier we become. Also, the more successful will we be in meeting every difficulty and testing time, whether at home or in business.

Many of our disasters are owing to our not meeting life and its experiences in the right way. Invariably, when we enquire into the cause of failure in a man's life, we find that he has for years been avoiding some duty or difficulty, often wilfully so, or has engaged in some practice which has led to his downfall. If then he declares that he is the victim of fate, he is only partly correct, because he himself has been the cause of his own failure, and he himself has been his own fate.

The only way fate can be avoided is by becoming changed, so that the painful experience becomes unnecessary.

The cause of our so-called fate, then, is within us, and we can master it only by ourselves becoming changed.

What is fate? It is in no sense a punishment, although it is partly the reaping of past sowing. It is a series of events attracted by our lack of certain qualities of character, which have made us think and act in a certain manner. For instance, one may be perfectly good in a negative sense that is, one may be free from all vices and sins, as generally understood – and yet lack certain of those positive qualities of character which are necessary to make up the complete character of the perfect man.

All who have passed through the great trials realise that they are the better for the experiences, and that it has been well worthwhile. They also see that if they had previously possessed the quality of character which they developed while passing through the trial, it would have been unnecessary for them to meet the experience at all.

It is a glorious truth that if we follow the light, we become changed. That we become entirely new creatures is not a mere figure of speech, but an actual and tremendous fact. As the years go by, we become changed, both in character and substance. In one sense, we are apparently the same. To the casual observer, we look much the same, we also bear the same name and may work at the same job; but to the observant, or those who know us intimately, there is a great change. We are not the same, because the old nature is dying, and the new nature is growing stronger day by day.

Gradually, our desires become transmuted. The things which once chained us to the earth no longer chain us. The powers which once enslaved us are broken one by one. No longer do we find any pleasure in sin. What used to attract us repels us. What used to give us pleasure fills us with disgust and horror. Actually, old things pass away, and all things become new.

The regenerate life is possible only as we keep our thoughts stayed upon God. If we continually look up, then the eternal regenerative life of the Spirit flows into us. Thus it is that we become changed.

One has not to be either learned or clever in order to enter the Kingdom of God. All that one has to do is to follow the teachings of Jesus Christ. This is very simple, yet it is too difficult, except for a mere handful in each generation. "Narrow is the way which leadeth unto life," said our Lord, "and few there be that find it."

To those who enter the path, there is only one law, and that is the law of love. Our Lord tells us what to do: to love God and man; to love our enemies and slanderers; never to retaliate; simply to love and resist not. Such teaching is mere foolishness to the natural man, but it contains the very essence of the inner truth to those who are in the path.

Those who are living the Christ life are on a different footing altogether from that of those still in the material consciousness. To the pilgrim, life consists of a series of wonderful experiences. These experiences are tests and initiations. They are necessary at the time to help us on our journey, and bring us into a deeper, richer and more intimate knowledge and understanding of God. If then we fight against them, we fight against God, and life, and our highest good. Always there comes to us the right experience that we need, just at the rightful time.

Life is made up of a series of experiences, all of which are, in a deep interior sense, the best for us at the time. When we have learned their lesson, they pass away. There is no mystery about it; everything works according to law. As soon as we are fit for better things, the opening comes, together with a call to go up higher. When we respond, we find that our experiences have been the best possible training for our new life of larger and more responsible service. The further we progress, the greater wisdom, fortitude, patience, stability and strength are demanded of us. Life is always calling for those who are willing to bear the burden, but very few are willing to take it up.

Our life is either good or evil according to the use we make of it. If we give in to difficulties, if we rebel against the discipline, if we choose the easier path instead of the harder, life becomes increasingly difficult and apparently evil. If, however, we choose the hard path of duty and self–discipline; if we expand our minds, enlarge our thoughts, increase our efficiency, and grow in mind and capacity, life becomes truly easier and very much smoother. So long as we let life whip us, we find it a hard taskmaster, and the more we kick, the worse things become. But when, by choosing the hardest tasks, we grow strong, life fawns at our feet.

It is the same with success. So long as we chase after it, it eludes us and mocks at us; but when we adopt the strong, victorious attitude, it runs after us instead.

A higher and more difficult and responsible place in life is always waiting for us, but we shall never find it until we are capable of filling it. We all find our own level sooner or later. Environment has no power; it simply reflects what we are within.

Life is spiritual, and environment is quite fluid. It simply reflects the state of the individual and provides him with an experience that is necessary at the time. No one is forced. Where mind and spirit lead, matter and environment have to follow.

While it is true that our lives are a reflection of what we are within, it is true also that we are, within, what our thoughts make us; therefore, our thoughts control our lives. Until we can guide our thoughts Godward, we are the victim of a vicious circle. We are what our thoughts make us, yet we think according to what we are.

It is hopeless so long as we leave the Spirit out of our calculations. If we are what we think, and if we think what we are, not knowing the truth, what hope have we? For we can never, of ourselves, think rightly. But all things are possible with the Spirit. In our ignorance, we seek for satisfaction in every way but the right one, and in things noble and things base, until at last the soul knows that satisfaction can never be found in any earthly thing at all.

Just at the right time, when humans have learned the great lesson that the things of senses and flesh and personality, no matter how good in themselves, can never satisfy the soul, a change takes place within. We desire to live after the Spirit instead of after the flesh or the senses.

At such times, we are led to certain books or teachings, apparently by sheer luck or chance. But later we will realise that we have been led by the Spirit to find just the teaching that we needed in the time of greatest need.

Henceforward, we are completely changed, for the new birth of the Spirit has taken place, and what is mystically called the Christ child is born within us, becoming our real higher self, guiding us ever upward.

Now the struggle begins. Although born again, the beginner is only a babe in Christ. He has to grow and develop. He has continually to put off the old man (old habits of thought chiefly) and put on the new. Old thought habits persist; old desires may rear their heads, but man can be victorious through the Christ within. He has patiently to reverse his thoughts and think no more of the flesh, or error, or limitation, or as though evil were a positive reality, but according to the Spirit—i.e., love, harmony, wholeness, perfection, faith, hope, courage, purity, and so on. With new hope in his heart, realising that he is a son of God, he lives a new life of ever-increasing beauty, true achievement and joy. He receives glimpses of absolute truth, which enable him, still further, to bring his thoughts, emotions, and actions into harmony with God's Mind, Will, Thought, and Idea.

The new human makes a study of right thinking. We learn to think God's thoughts after Him—to think from the standpoint of eternal truth, instead of from that of human error. We meditate no longer upon sin and imperfection, but upon the Divine idea or word, the Logos.

Through the Spirit, then, we become altered, our thoughts become changed, our lives become transformed.

Chapter Two

A New Commandment

"A new commandment I give unto you, that ye love one another; as I have loved you, that ye also love one another."

"As the Father hath loved me, so have I loved you: continue ye in my love."

If ye keep my commandments, ye shall abide in my love; even as I have kept my Father's commandments, and abide in His love."

"This is my commandment, that ye love one another, as I have loved you."

In this twentieth century since this new commandment was given to the world, it is as new as ever. It remains new simply because it is still unused and ignored by the majority of humankind. Only a handful out of each generation has dared to put the teaching of Jesus into practice. As far as the masses are concerned, the new commandment of Jesus is unknown – or, at any rate, unnoticed and untried.

Jesus Christ came to reveal to the world the character of God, and this can be summed up in one word: love. There was no other way whereby humanity could be saved than by this revelation of Divine Love. In the life, teaching and crucifixion of our Lord, we see the infinite Love of God laid bare, for it reveals Love to the uttermost – even to death and the ignominy of the cross.

This is how Christ has loved us – and we are to love one another, even as He has loved us.

> "Greater love hath no one than this, that a person lay down their life for their friends."

We are to love others even as Christ has loved us – He who gave His life a ransom for many.

No wonder the world has shunned and slighted the new commandment of Jesus. Yet obedience to it is the only way whereby the world can be saved. It is also the only way by which we can prove that we are children of God.

The Christian religion is essentially simple – so simple that even a child may grasp it. If we love our fellow human beings, even as

Christ has loved us, we are His disciples. But if we do not love in this way, we are not.

> "Ye shall know the tree by its fruits. Do people gather grapes from thorns, or figs from thistles?"

O people, weary of complicated theologies and the strife of creeds, give heed to the simple truth of the simplest of all religions – that of Christ. Listen to the words of the beloved disciple:

> "Again, a new commandment I write unto you, which thing is true in him and in you: because the darkness is past, and the true light now shines."

> "The one who says they are in the light, and hates their sibling, is in darkness even until now."

> "The one who loveth their sibling abides in the light, and there is no occasion of stumbling in them."

> "But the one who hates their sibling is in darkness, and walks in darkness, and knows not where they go, because that darkness has blinded their eyes."

Many people are so confused at the present time that they do not know what to believe. The teachings of the churches are so contradictory they would puzzle even a philosopher. But these complications may be set aside if we listen to the simple teaching of the Lord Jesus and of St John, which shows us at once where we are.

If we love others, even as Christ has loved us – unselfishly, giving ourselves entirely, hoping for no reward – we belong to the Lord of Love. If, however, we do not love others in this way, or bear hate, malice or resentment, we are none of His.

There is no room for complicated theories and theologies in the religion of Christ. It is possible for a child, entirely ignorant of doctrine or theological theories and subtleties, to enter the Kingdom by learning to love others, even as Christ has loved us.

> "If ye keep my commandments, ye shall abide in my love."

> "This is my commandment: that ye love one another."

It is so simple – yet it demands so much of each one of us that few are prepared to respond. Many will say:

> "How can we love in the same way that Christ has loved us? We are not capable of loving to the same extent as God, who is Love itself."

True – but we can love in the same way, even if not to the same extent.

- We can love others instead of self.

- We can serve our day and generation instead of doing everything for gain.

- We can follow the Golden Rule in all our dealings.

- We can live peaceably with all.

- We can use "the soft answer that turneth away wrath".

In spite of our failures and shortcomings, we can follow the gleam. Even though we follow afar off – faint, yet pursuing – we are still disciples of the Lord of Love, belonging to Him and abiding in His love.

But we cannot be satisfied with following afar off. How then can we attain to "the measure of the stature of the fullness of Christ"? The great secret is a changed inner thought life. "Ye must be born again" – of the Spirit.

Our thoughts must become spiritualised – must be brought into captivity to Christ, the Lord of Love. Thought precedes all action – therefore, all our thoughts must be led captive by love.

But our thoughts are dependent upon something deeper. This deeper "something" is the dominant idea around which our thoughts revolve. If this dominant idea is self, then our thoughts will be selfish and our actions antagonistic.

If the dominant idea is love, even as Christ has loved us, then all our thoughts will be love-thoughts, and all our actions a reflection – feeble though it may be – of the life of Christ.

How then can this inward dominant idea be changed? "Ye must be born again." It is the work of the Spirit.

We, of ourselves, cannot change our inward dominant idea. But in the life of each of us comes a time when the Spirit of Truth – often through circumstances – strives with us gently, endeavouring to persuade us to give up self and surrender entirely to the Love Principle, or Lord of Love.

When this wonderful awakening takes place, and the Spirit pulls at our heartstrings, we are indeed wise if we surrender entirely to Love.

If we do this, the dominant idea becomes changed. The centre around which our thoughts revolve is shifted – brought into alignment with the Divine Centre of all.

But if we do not make this surrender – if we resist the Spirit's influence – we cut ourselves off from the Eternal Life of God, becoming spiritually bankrupt, and separated in consciousness entirely from God.

But if we surrender unto Love, what then?

> "Beloved, now are we the children of God."

As children of God, our lives become attuned to the Divine Order, and all our thoughts brought into harmony with the Law of Love.

Then we find the results of our true thinking made manifest in our life. The fruits of the Spirit will show in our character, and His joy will be in us.

It is only in this way that harmony and peace can be brought to this sad and disordered world.

> "For the earnest expectation of the creation waits for the manifestation of the children of God."

The world is to be saved by the children of God, who shall reflect the Love of Christ. Love is the only power that can win the hearts of people.

Threats of eternal damnation have always failed to win souls to Christ – but love has never failed when given a fair opportunity.

The children of God must reflect the love of Christ if the world is to be saved from itself. They must be willing to lay down their lives, if necessary, so that others may be won to Love Divine.

Therefore, the call comes to us all – to follow the Lord of Love, to surrender entirely to the Love Principle, to bring every thought into captivity to Christ, and to love one another, even as He has loved us.

CHAPTER THREE

The Love Which Passeth Knowledge

Our blessed Lord's teaching might be described as two-fold – the Kingdom, and how to find it. What the Kingdom *is* was never explained. It was likened in parable to many things, but what it *is* could not and never can be described in human language. It is something that can be found and experienced; but those who find can never describe what it is. It is past all describing, but it is not past finding – for there is a way to this Kingdom, and it is made so simple that "wayfaring men, though fools, shall not err therein".

The Kingdom of God is the realm of Divine order and is Divine order itself. But this perfect order is due to the fact that it is the outcome of Love. Divine order is Divine love in expression. The realm of Divine order, or Heaven, is what it is solely because it is Love, perfectly expressed. The delightfully harmonious and orderly state which constitutes Heaven is all due to the fact that Divine love meets with no hindrance. All the denizens of Heaven vie with one another in expressing love with ever greater perfection, if such a thing be possible. They are always trying to serve in love, more and more, considering how they can make others happy with a complete forgetfulness of self; while all combine in a great consuming passion for the Lord, the Divine Fountain of all love. Therefore, the Kingdom of Heaven is the Kingdom of Love. The Kingdom of Heaven is the Kingdom of God and His righteousness or Divine order. Therefore, because God is love, the Kingdom of Heaven is the Kingdom of Love.

I have put it in this crude form in order to make the subject simple to all. It does not explain, however, what Jesus meant by the term "the Kingdom of Heaven". But it gives us the key by which we may find entrance. If the Kingdom of God is the Kingdom of Love, then the entrance to it is love.

What we are all seeking is Divine union, although we may not all be aware of it. Nothing less than this will, or can, ever satisfy us. "Thou hast created us for Thyself, and our hearts can find no rest until they find it in Thee." It is only as God dwells in us, and we in Him, that we can find ease for our pain, and satisfaction of our desire.

But how can we find this Divine union in which God dwells in us and we in Him so that we become one? Many are the ways and methods that are offered to the budding aspirant, but the simple way is that of Love. Love is the key – the open sesame – to that perfect union which alone can satisfy the deep longings of our soul, and which alone can fill us with unspeakable joy and bliss. "God is love; and he that dwelleth in love, dwelleth in God, and God in him", said the Spirit through the inspired and sanctified St

John. Here then is the key – to dwell in Love, for if we do so, God dwells in us, and we dwell in Him; and so, to the extent that we dwell in love, do we partake of a state of union with the Divine.

If we are to make any progress in the Pilgrim journey, we must abide in love – we must be love itself. We must walk in Love's way if ever we are to enter the Kingdom of God. What a light this statement of St John throws upon the statement of our Lord, that the greatest commandment is that we should love the Lord our God with all our heart, and with all our soul, and with all our mind; and that like unto it is the command that we must love our neighbour as our own self. On these two commandments hang all the law and the prophets. And to the lawyer who questioned Him, our Lord said: "This do and thou shalt live." There was no difficult doctrine to be believed, or understood, no occult attainment to be mastered – simply that if he fulfilled and obeyed these commandments, he would live – that is, he would enter into eternal life.

But the lawyer wanted to excuse himself, so Jesus told the parable of the Good Samaritan, and then asked of this questioner, which of the ones mentioned was neighbour to the man who fell among thieves? And he replied: "He that showed mercy on him." Then Jesus said: "Go thou and do likewise."

So we see that this is a true, sure and simple way, leading directly to the Kingdom of Eternal Life – to love God and our neighbour and to show mercy – in other words, to be love itself, to love one another, and so fulfil the law of Christ.

But some may say: this is only the old Jewish law and is not Christianity at all. It may be, but it is the teaching of Jesus Christ, who said: "Think not that I am come to destroy the law, or the prophets: I am come not to destroy, but to fulfil." The law of love had been previously given to people, but it was not followed or understood in all its fullness. Jesus came to fulfil it – to be love, even to His death on the cross – to reveal what love is, and to show us what we have to be if we are to be His real disciples.

Jesus brought a new conception of love to the world – a new conception of the love of God to us, in that He sent His own Son; and of the love of people to God, and of people to one another. And in this teaching, He shows us the way to complete unity or at–oneness, and, through this, to complete liberation and freedom. Until we become love in thought, desire, motive, word and actions, we are mere plague spots or festering sores in the Cosmic body: we are centres of discord and disharmony. But when we become love, and love our fellow beings and the good Father of all, we come into harmony and unity with the whole, thus becoming one. And so unity and oneness, from which we have by nature fallen, is at length restored.

Relief it is, to many of us who have theological difficulties, to find such a simple gospel, and to find also that it is the teaching of our Lord Himself, backed up by the disciple who loved Him most and who understood Him best. We gladly admit that there are other doctrines than this in the New Testament; but this way of approach is complete, and those who cannot accept other doctrines can find in it all that they need. No great intelligence or intellectual power is required – simply the heart and mind of a little child. All are invited to enter this path. It is not strait because any are excluded; it is only strait because we are so reluctant to love and forgive. For this call to God by the way of Jesus Christ is not a matter of intellect. Intellectual assent to it, as a doctrine, will never admit anyone into the Kingdom of Love. The only entrance is through becoming love itself. It is not what we believe, but what we are, and do, that matters. We may think all sorts of beautiful things about God, but unless we ourselves become all these beautiful things, it avails nothing.

> "Not everyone that saith unto me, Lord, Lord, shall enter into the Kingdom of Heaven, but he that doeth the will of my Father Which is in Heaven. For many will say to me in that day, Lord, Lord, have we not prophesied in Thy name? And in Thy name have cast out devils? And in Thy name done many wonderful works? And then will I profess unto them, I never knew you: depart from me, ye that work iniquity. Therefore, whosoever heareth these sayings of mine, and doeth them, I will liken him unto a wise man which built his house upon a rock: and the rain descended, and the floods came, and the winds blew, and beat upon that house; and it fell not: for it was founded upon a rock."
>
> Matthew 7:21

We have, therefore, to be, and not merely to believe; we have to do, and not merely to hear the teaching of love. It is not sufficient that we think fine thoughts or speak and talk beautifully about love. We have to become love itself – we have to be love in all that we think, say, and do.

Those who begin to live the life of love – who earnestly desire to become love itself, even as He is love – soon discover that they have entered a course of training. They find that they have to pass through certain initiations: not the initiations of mysterious occultism, but tests of love. Soon they meet with an experience that proves whether they have any real love in them, or only mere talk and theory. They are liable to be upset by this and to think that either they have gone wrong or that love is not the underlying principle, after all. But we can become love itself only through becoming changed into love. And this change is wrought through experience. Each incident, as it arises, is an opportunity for us to show that we are love, and to demonstrate that there is real love in us: not perfectly expressed, perhaps, but still present, nevertheless.

Judging by my correspondence, many people have imperfect ideas of love. They say that they cannot love dirty tramps, criminals, harlots, cheats, etc. They seem to think that loving means putting their arms around other people's necks and kissing them. But if they were to think of love as goodwill, friendliness, mercy, long-suffering, kindness, forgiveness, etc., they would soon realise what true universal love is, until they reach the stage when they yearn over humanity just as much as they yearn over their own child.

The first thing, probably, that we have to learn is to forgive. So simple, yet so difficult. It is difficult because what hurts us always seems such an injustice. But we have to learn to forgive, no matter how unjustly we have been treated. There can be no entrance to the Kingdom, neither can we make any advancement in the spiritual path, if we cannot forgive those who have wronged us. But, thank God, if we forgive, freely and utterly, those who have wronged us, then we can go forward in that path which leads to the fulfilment of all our deepest longings and desires. This is why our Lord taught that if we forgive others their wrongs to us, God also will forgive us the wrongs we have done to Him. God is all love and forgiveness, but we cannot enter into His love, neither can we enjoy His forgiveness, until we forgive those who have wronged us. God, who is love, yearns and longs to have every one of us, but cannot admit into the Kingdom of Love those who are not love, and who are so far from being love itself, as not to forgive those who have injured and wronged them.

But we have not only to forgive those who have really wronged us, we must also forgive those who have merely annoyed us, and "rubbed us up the wrong way". Even a cat does not like being stroked the wrong way, and the fur of black cats, so it is said, emits sparks of electricity when this is done. I am afraid that we human beings are much the same. But we must learn to forgive all who vex and try us, for it is only through this gate of forgiveness that we can enter into liberty.

But all this, after all, is only the negative side of the subject. We have not only to forgive and to give up all resentment, but also we must obey the injunction: "Love your enemies, bless them that curse you, do good to them that hate you, and pray for them that despitefully use you, and persecute you; that ye may be the children of your Father which is in heaven." But "doing good" to our enemies must not be a painful duty, but a true act of love. We have to be love, genuinely and truly, if we are to be children of the One who is Love itself.

Now, how can all this be brought about? How are we to forgive and to love and do good, instead of nursing our anger and resentment, and brooding over our wrongs? The great secret is to surrender to the Lord of Love. He is always knocking at our heart's door: He is forever in our soul, saying: "My child, give me thy heart." Surrendering to Love makes Love's ways easy, or, at any rate, possible of achievement. If we respond to the Divine Love, then it becomes comparatively easy to be loving to others.

In the days of my youth, and before, people preached hell–fire to the masses. Many may have been frightened thereby into repentance, but it must have been the love of God revealed in Jesus Christ that softened or broke their hearts, making them new creatures. It is only love that can save: it is only love that can reconcile humanity to God. God does not need to be reconciled to humanity, but humanity needs to be reconciled to God, and

Divine love is the only power that can accomplish this. If the world is to be saved, it is only love that can accomplish it. No appeal to self-interest can ever win people to God, but only the love of God, breaking down their hardness and lack of love, their selfishness and enmity, until their hearts and minds become like those of a little child.

It is only the love of God which can soften our hearts. We love Him because He first loved us.

But there is a way whereby we can the more effectively put love into action, thus gaining the victory. We may feel that we cannot forgive, yet if we follow this simple technique, it becomes possible of achievement, in time. Of course, we should pray that our heart may be softened, and that we may be able to love, where now we hate or dislike. This is taken for granted. Then, in our quiet time set apart for prayer and subjective reflection, we should direct our thoughts to the one who has upset us, and say, audibly, "So-and-so, I forgive you freely." It may seem too simple to be of any use, but, if it is persevered with, it will make a real and full forgiveness possible.

In course of time, we can go a step further, when we feel that we really have forgiven our adversary, and say: "So-and-so, I forgive you and love you. Go in peace." This, too, may occasion some trouble, but after a time it becomes an accomplished fact. And then, finally, we can go yet another step further, and pray for our late adversary, that they may be blessed in every possible way, even as we would that our nearest and dearest should be blessed. By persevering in this way, we find that we can pray for our enemies and yearn over them just as much as for our best friend; and in so doing, the last chain is broken asunder, and we become free.

Then we discover that the experience has been a glorious help up in the spiritual life, advancing us and speeding us towards that blessed state when we are changed into the likeness of the Beloved – when we become even as love itself.

We should never let the sun go down on our wrath. We should never retire to sleep until we have entered into liberty and peace through forgiving, loving, and praying for all who have hurt us, wronged us, or upset us in any way during the day. We may feel that we do not want to be bothered, that we want to forget rather than to forgive. This slothfulness must be overcome, for it is only in this way that we can become true followers and disciples of the Lord of Love.

If we make a habit of nightly reviewing the incidents of the day – dragging out any unpleasant incident that may have occurred and resolving it all in love, mercy, and forgiveness – we can retire in peace and joy and bliss, such as we could never experience otherwise.

CHAPTER FOUR

Living the Harmonious Life

The truly harmonious life can be lived and enjoyed only by those who are led by the Spirit. The way of the Spirit is harmony and peace. There is no friction, struggle, difficulty, disharmony or disorder in the Spirit. When the time is ripe, all things work together and fit into their places like the various parts of a well-oiled machine, entirely without effort or strain. Just at the right moment the right thing comes to pass – something or someone comes to us, other things are moved aside, and everything slips into its place as easily as the fitting together of a puzzle that has been correctly assembled.

As we look over the universe, we see order and precision everywhere. In spite of its complexity, it is marvellously simple. In spite of the fact that everything is in motion, there are no hitches. There are no traffic blocks in the cosmos – no mistakes made to cause confusion and disorder. One heavenly body does not arrive too early; another does not arrive too late. Everything is in its right place at the right time. The whole universe works smoothly, following a Master Plan, obeying a Master Law.

The way of the Spirit is like unto this, but is harmonious to a finer and higher degree. As in the visible universe, there is a Master Plan being unfolded with utmost smoothness and delightful harmony. All disharmony in our life is due to the fact that we are not in correspondence with the inner spiritual plan or motif.

There is no disharmony in the Spirit, but only the most exquisite order. It is only as we come into correspondence with this inner Divine Order that our life can become filled with harmony and peace.

If, in the visible universe, one sun were to go out of its course, what terrible confusion and disorder would result. We imagine that, in course of time, it would wreck the whole system. In the same way, because we have departed from our true spiritual orbit, our life is filled with disorder. Harmony can be restored only by our being brought into the perfect Divine Orbit designed for us in the Mind of God.

Disharmony is humankind's constant companion because we do not live in harmony with Divine Law and because we do not follow the Divine Plan of our life or travel our true orbit. The teaching of our Lord — that we should love God with all our might, and our fellow human beings as much as ourselves — if followed, brings us into correspondence with the Divine Harmony. One can easily see that if all the world were to practise this teaching, harmony and peace would be at once established. It would abolish selfishness, greed, jealousy, envy, distrust and all the things which cause war and disorder.

The first essential is that we should obey this teaching ourselves instead of worrying because other people do not follow it. When we have learnt to love God and our fellow human beings, we find that we possess an increasing desire to do the will of God. In endeavouring to do the will of God, we are obeying the teaching of our Lord: "Not everyone that sayeth unto me, Lord, Lord, shall enter into the Kingdom of Heaven; but he that doeth the will of my Father which is in Heaven".

The outstanding characteristic of Heaven — that true world which is the perfect expression of the Divine Idea — is a delightful harmony due to everyone doing the will of God perfectly.

Indeed, it is because the two lines of conduct taught by our Lord are followed in Heaven that Heaven is what it is. Every inhabitant of Heaven loves God with their whole heart, soul, mind and strength, and others as themselves. Their great delight is to serve and love and bless others, and their chief happiness to do the will of God. This constitutes Heaven, and our Lord, by giving us this teaching, tells us how to bring Heaven to earth — to establish the Kingdom of God here in our hearts and lives now.

Incidentally, it may be mentioned that it is only by following the teaching of Christ – instead of merely talking about it – that civilisation can be saved from self-destruction. Love, forgiveness, goodwill – the Christ spirit – put into practical expression, can alone save humanity.

Doing the will of God. How repellent it is to us in our early stages, but what a joy as we advance farther along the Path of the New Life! After a time, the only thing that can bring us joy and happiness – that can satisfy the longing of our soul — is doing the will of God.

At first, we fear where it may lead us. It is a fearful thing, we think, to fall into the hands of the living God. But when we have taken the plunge, we find that it is all love, and that doing the will of God leads to victory and glories such as cannot be described.

"Yes", some may say, "doing the will of God brought our Lord to the cross on which He was nailed, and it also brought many of His followers to a martyr's end — tortured, sawn asunder, thrown to the lions – all through doing the will of God. There is surely no happiness or peace about such experiences as these?" The answer to this is that our Lord incarnated specially in order that this thing might be done to Him, and if He had not done the will of His Father, His mission would have failed. His apparent failure was our Lord's greatest victory. The apparent success of the powers of evil was really their complete defeat and humiliation. They were allowed to do their worst – and when they had done it, they had but given our Lord the greatest victory that has ever been known.

In a similar way were the martyrs, though in a lesser degree, saviours of the world. It was their high destiny to suffer for their Lord's cause and to bear witness to the Truth. By their sacrifice, they prepared the way for those who followed. If they had not remained faithful, even to the extent of giving their lives, theirs would have been utter failure. Their seeming failure was their greatest victory. The martyr's crown will surely shine the brightest among the redeemed of Heaven.

We are likewise called to follow our Lord to the uttermost – to do the will though it may lead to persecution, or even to torture. In it and through it we will find joy unspeakable and happiness and peace.

> "Blessed are ye when men shall revile you, and persecute you, and say all manner of evil against you, falsely, for my sake. Rejoice, and be exceeding glad, for great is your reward in Heaven, for so persecuted they the prophets which were before you."
>
> Matthew 5:11-12

No matter what we may be called upon to do in this life, it is only by doing the will of God that we can live in harmony, peace, joy and happiness. If we are called to persecution, then only by obeying that call can we find harmony, peace and joy. If we disobey, we are of all people the most miserable and wretched – we join the ranks of the Judas class, whose greatest anguish is in thinking of what might have been. So near to the Kingdom, but alas, faithless in the hour of supreme test.

Harmony, peace and joy can only be won through doing the will of God – no matter where it may lead.

If we earnestly so desire, following Christ – who is at once the perfect archetype and the most glorious flower of humanity – everything will work together for good. All seeming evil and difficulty only serve to help us in our spiritual journey. Gradually, the shackles fall away from us. Envy, sensuality, harmful habits, selfishness, love of ease, appetite, hate – all are in turn overcome and vanquished. In their place appear the flowers of love, purity, and unselfishness – not in our own strength, but in the strength of Christ, who is always with us and dwells in us by the Spirit.

Doing the will of God is a glorious and beautiful experience. It is not the negative thing it is generally represented to be. We do not have to bow to God's will so much as rise to it, to enjoy it, to rejoice in it, to live it.

All this – and it is rather a long journey – leads up to the time when we are ready to be led by the Spirit entirely. This is an advanced stage of the spiritual life. First, there is striving and effort; the constant warfare and the passing through many experiences and tests. There comes a time, however, when we turn the corner, after which God works the Divine Plan out in and through us, and we are led by the Spirit entirely.

One who is led entirely by the Spirit lives in a heaven of peace and quietness. The fret and fever of life do not affect them. They are "content to let the world go by; to know no gain or loss". Therefore, most of the things which vex and grieve the hearts of others cannot affect them. Most of the pain and suffering of life comes through attachment to things. A person may be heartbroken at the loss of a valuable pearl necklace; another may be deeply hurt because they were omitted from an honours list. But to one who is non-attached, these things mean little – no more than diamonds or gold to someone dying of hunger and thirst on a desert island.

Suffering, disappointment, and pain are generally due to desire being directed towards earthly and worldly things. When we are led by the Spirit, our desire is for spiritual things. We no longer yearn for the baubles of life but seek the riches that fade not away. After a time, this brings us into peace – the peace that passes human understanding. We may be considered an object of contempt by the world, but this does not trouble us, for we possess inward peace and true harmony. This more than satisfies.

There is nothing so easy or simple as being led by the Spirit, yet at the same time, nothing so difficult. So simple to talk about – so difficult to follow. "How can I know that I am being led by the Spirit?" is the beginner's constant question. Each one seeking must find out for themselves.

It is a matter of testing through experience. But the time comes to the earnest seeker when they can feel whether they are working in harmony with the Spirit or whether they are out of harmony. When the right step is taken, a peace and spiritual joy will usually be felt, but a wrong step will be followed by restlessness and discomfort, which will not cease until that step is retraced and a wise decision made.

Great indeed is the perplexity of those who begin to live the spiritual life. They wish to be guided by the Spirit, but they do not yet have the certainty of experience. The only way is to be bold, to make decisions, and to experiment – carefully noting the results. But a good rule is, when in doubt, to wait. Then, gradually, light will come, along with increasing confidence, so that decisions of the greatest importance can be made firmly and promptly.

Beginners may exclaim despairingly: "This is all so far advanced – I cannot hope to follow. What shall I do?" Here is a simple prescription. First, choose always to do what is right, avoiding what you know to be wrong or second best. Follow Christ, believing that the Spirit is always at hand to help and bless. Choose always that course which is best for the world and for your highest inward good. Pray always. If you follow Truth in this way, greater light will come to you.

Chapter Five

The Life Victorious

A favourite quotation has been that from Phillips Brooks: "Do not pray for easy lives; pray to be stronger men. Do not pray for tasks equal to your powers; pray for strength equal to your tasks." In this counsel is to be found the secret of the victorious life. One who follows it develops the only right attitude of mind. And we will find that our life is simplified by our choosing that which is apparently difficult. Here we find one of life's great paradoxes: if we seek an easier life, then our life, realised in experience, becomes more difficult every day. On the contrary, if we choose the difficult and heroic path, our life will simplify, becoming actually easier and smoother.

Who then is bound for the Kingdom – who is willing to set out on the great adventure? The Spirit chooses heroic souls. There is no place in these ranks for those inclined to spiritual indolence who wish to live easily. "Many are called, but few are chosen." But everyone is accepted who is willing to choose the more difficult path, praying for strength equal to the task ahead, instead of whining and pleading for an easier existence.

In these noble words of Phillips Brooks, we may realise that there is always strength available, equal to every need. If we choose that which is right and follow on, no matter where it may lead, or what it may cost – even as Christ did – we will be helped by invisible forces, knowing also that victory is of the Lord.

Many of us are afraid to trust ourselves to the great adventure because we have not yet got our thoughts right and clear about God. We are afraid to venture all because we dare not trust God. We do not have sufficient confidence in Him. We look at the world and judge by appearances. We discover apparent disorder and imperfection in nature; we see worse disorder and evil in the life of humanity; we stand at the bedside, perhaps, of someone dying of cancer; and then we say – "God is not able to control His own universe; therefore, how can we trust Him?"

If we allow ourselves to judge by appearances, we can never make any progress in the spiritual life. We have to believe in God — omnipotent, all-loving, and all-wise — and trust Him, in spite of appearances.

Again, many of us are afraid to trust God because we fear that He is a God of hate and revenge. One reader once wrote to say that, owing to her upbringing, she was afraid to say, "Thy will be done," for fear that God would throw her into Hell. But God is a God of love and compassion. He does not punish us, in reality; we simply punish ourselves by remaining outside His love. It is true that we suffer much if we refuse to respond to the love of God and fail to harmonise with it. But this is not the fault of Love. The more that

Love loves, the more painful it is for us if we do not respond and if we are not in harmony. This certainly is not the fault of Love. Love can only love – and if we respond and get into correspondence with it, we find joy unspeakable, and harmony and peace. But we have to trust God in order to find Him. We have to give Him credit for being at least as loving, just and trustworthy as ourselves. We can make no progress in spiritual things until we learn to trust and have confidence in God.

Others of us fear, perhaps, to venture out on the great journey of the soul because we are afraid of the power of evil. We are afraid to trust God because we doubt whether He is capable of protecting us from the power of evil that seems greater than the power of good.

We are miserable and live in fear and trembling because of the evil that may attack us next. Many of us believe in evil more than we do in God. We do not believe in an omnipotent God, but rather One who has let His universe get out of hand, so that He can no longer control it. We have to give up all this wrong thinking. God is omnipotent and quite capable of looking after His universe. And this is the right thought – seeing through appearance – that we have to instil into our consciousness. Evil, whatever it may seem, has got no upper hand. There is a controlling Power at work, and all things are overruled for good, in spite of humanity's failure in cooperation.

Again, many fear to venture lest they be submerged. The path of high adventure, they think, is too difficult and hazardous. The dangers, difficulties, the tests – so many, so great, so severe. How can they hope to be victorious? Better stay in the valley, they think, than perish on the heights. This is the age-long mistake.

We have to venture all if we are to gain all; we have to lose our life if we would save it.

We must learn to see through appearances, obey the promptings of the heart, listen to the voice of intuition, and thereby also attain to revelation.

The life of high adventure has its foundation amid the common things of life. In our experiences – the trials and difficulties – is hidden the secret of a greater and more abundant life. However cheerless and prosaic our duty may seem, in it and through it runs the way of eternal and glorious life. In the last book of the Bible, it is stated that to them that overcome, the most wonderful things are given – and which make us marvel as we read. Yet the promise is only to those who overcome. And the overcoming has its roots in our everyday life, amid those very difficulties and trials from which often we have prayed to be released. But the prayer of the overcomer must be, not to be relieved from our troubles, but that strength be given so that our trials and difficulties may be overcome.

Some of us may be inclined to think that if only these hindering troubles, limitations and difficulties were removed, we could then live a grand life of victory, in which we should accomplish great and noble things. Nothing is further from the truth. If we cannot overcome in the little things, how can we accomplish great things?

It is only when we have overcome in the circumstances in which we are now placed – it is only when we have proved ourselves worthy in our present conditions – that we can be chosen or promoted to higher and greater service.

That we overcome now, in everyday things, is the all-important matter. Our difficulties, limitations and troubles are of far greater importance than we think. If we try to shirk them, then life becomes increasingly difficult, and we never find the path to the Kingdom of God. There is no room for shirkers in the Kingdom of Heaven – only for those who have proved themselves worthy. Many are called, but few are chosen. The worthy and faithful ones only are chosen, for they alone are capable of bearing the tremendous responsibilities that will have to be undertaken later. If the one with five talents had not been faithful to the extent of five talents, it is obvious that they would never have been reliable enough to be entrusted with the rule and care of five cities.

But how can we overcome? How can we become stronger than our tasks?

Firstly, we must realise God as omnipotent in our life and destiny as well as in the universe, in the larger sense. Evil, or what is called the power of evil, cannot in any way hurt those who have given themselves unto God. It is those whose lives are separate from God who are vulnerable. And those who follow evil, allowing evil thoughts to occupy their minds – whose thoughts have not been brought into captivity to Christ, for that they believe in Evil rather than in Good – such lay themselves ever open to evil and negative influences. Nevertheless, there is always a Divine Power which acts as a restraint and keeps all things within certain bounds.

But those who refuse to judge by appearances, stoutly affirming that God is Good and Love, who take their stand in Truth, putting themselves utterly in the Divine care – they can never be overcome by the powers of evil. Only good can come to them, because everything is overruled for good. There is no evil purpose in life, but only love. The only evil is in yielding to temptation, or sin, and thus living apart from God.

Now, if these things are true – and indeed they are – why should we hesitate or falter in the way of life? And why should we pray for our difficulties to be removed, for our life to be made easier, or for an easy transition to the next life? And if they are true – as gloriously true they are – why be filled with forebodings and fears, doubts and unbeliefs?

There is but one thing to be done – to press on, trusting in Divine Love, Care and Guidance, unto victory and all that it means. Our great Elder Brother has blazed the trail before us, that we may follow Him.

There are those who, through deprivation, or bereavement or failure, feel stunned and helpless amid the wreckage of their happiness. For these ones who despair, is this new effort, this further journey, worthwhile?

Yes, yes, a thousand times yes. The sun is shining on the Hills of God. Come up out of the dark valley and the night of your mourning shall be ended. Come, brother, come, sister – let us tread once more the heavenly steeps that lead ever upwards to the City of God.

Ah, yes! It is well worthwhile. The road may appear to be utterly hopeless, cheerless and terribly difficult and lonely – but there are joys unspeakable, rest and peace for the soul, and comfort for bleeding hearts awaiting all those who will "take heart again" and go forward in the strength of their ever–present Lord.

Life seems so hopeless to us when we are in deep trouble, especially severe bereavement. This is only natural, but there is great help to be derived from directing the thoughts away from our own grief or trouble to the griefs or troubles of others. One can say: "Well, if I cannot be happy myself, I will try to make others happy. I shall not come this way again; therefore, I will make use of every opportunity of helping others." Many people have been saved from despair through having had to arouse themselves in order to keep things going for others dependent upon them.

In times of trouble and in the days of very small things, it is not easy to see that our ultimate victory, and the glorious future ensuing, depend upon our rising above our present difficulties. No matter how irksome the task before us, resisting the temptation to shirk it, let us do it gladly – or at least willingly and resolutely – so taking up our cross.

One may be galled by their present restricted life and its limitations, thinking perhaps that if they became a missionary, they could perform some great and noble work. They are mistaken. They would find life just the same – full of the same difficulties, annoyances and unpleasant duties. Each one must overcome their present difficulties – in other words, themselves – ere they may enter a higher and more responsible service.

Temptation cannot be overcome by fighting it, but simply by turning away from it to Christ, acknowledging that we ourselves are helpless, but that He is able to keep us from falling, and to transmute the lower into the higher. Not fighting, not killing, but transmutation is the secret of overcoming. No one who keeps their face turned towards the light can ever fail ultimately.

But some may say: "I do not understand. I have had no early training in spiritual things. What do you mean by Christ, and how can I look toward Him, or the light?" All we need is to acknowledge a power or presence of good that is far greater than our own. By this trusting in the good beyond ourselves, we find Christ ever at hand to help us in our need. His presence is with us, and His Spirit goes before us, preparing the way.

It is by overcoming the self that one overcomes the world and all its difficulties. In losing our "self", which is but a shadow on the screen of time, we find the one eternal self. It is by surrender that we find victory; it is by losing our life that we save it; it is in our weakness that we find strength; it is by giving all that we gain all.

He goes before; we follow on. Like unto the grain of mustard seed, our life victorious finds its origin in that which is very small and insignificant, but grows into a mighty and wonderful thing, as time unfolds.

Come, brother; come, sister – let us be up and doing. Let us go forward, and with all our power, strive to live the life victorious.

> Oh Christ, Thou Son of God,
> Thou One Eternal Self,
> Live Thou Thy life in me,
> Do Thou Thy will in me,
> Be Thou made flesh in me,
> I have no will but Thine,
> I have no self but Thee.

CHAPTER SIX

The More Abundant Life

Our Lord said, "I am come that they might have life, and that they might have it more abundantly". Christ came to give us a life that is more abundant, because it is real and eternal. He came with a Divine Attraction, that we might withdraw our affections from the things of the senses and of this world and set them on the things which are eternal. He came with persuasion and invitation, that we might give up the false life which is but a shadow on the screen of time, and enter into His own life, the eternal life of God, which is full and rich indeed – the Life of the Ages.

One stands, in this present life, at the parting of the ways. There comes a time in one's experience when a choice must be made between the things which are real and eternal, and those that are, after all, mere shadows and therefore cannot endure.

A person can either go with the stream of time and fate, or battle bravely towards a definite and eternal shore. One does not fall into this Divine Life by accident, nor can they enter through professing belief in a certain formula, or by intellectual faith – which is often inherited and does not touch the deeper springs of life. Eternal life has to be won. There is nothing in this world worth having for which we do not have to strive and make sacrifice. How much more so with this greatest thing of all, of which we must prove ourselves worthy.

Our Lord came to show us how to find the way, how to pursue the course, how to reach the goal. He took the journey Himself, clad in human weakness, in order to open the way for us – becoming not merely the Way-shower, but the very Way itself.

Firstly, the effect of our Lord's life is to draw our affections away from the love of self unto Himself. Loving Him, we love God – for "I and my Father are one". And this is available to the simplest person, for love is a matter of the heart and will, and not of the mind and intellect. But this also is required: "If you love me, keep my commandments".

We must be willing to give up all for His sake; we must hold back nothing. And this is the way of the Cross. It is the sure path to the larger, fuller, richer, more abundant life.

> All through life I see a cross
> Where sons of God yield up their breath;
> There is no gain except by loss,
> There is no Life except by death.

Our Lord captures not only our love, but our desires. We no longer desire the pomp and vanity of the world, but rather that which is pure and lovely. We no longer say, "What can I get?" or "What do I get out of it?" but "What can I give?" and "How can I serve?" This change of desire – or of heart – is a proof of the fact that we have been born again of the Spirit.

"How does this bring us into eternal life?" it may be asked. It does so because the change within us directs our will and our thoughts Godwards. It is by doing the Will that we enter the Life. "Not everyone that saith unto me, Lord, Lord, shall enter into the Kingdom of Heaven; but he that doeth the will of My Father which is in Heaven".

Human beings are in correspondence with their Divine Source only when their will is directed Godwards. When a person has been born again of the Spirit, they have one overmastering desire – to know God and be brought into complete harmony with the Divine. They want their own will to be moulded entirely after the Divine Pattern; they desire more than anything else that their will should conform to God's will – that they become one.

The Life of Attainment consists of a long journey, during which repeated adjustments and readjustments to the Divine Will have to be made. Time after time we may think, after a fresh and, apparently, final adjustment or surrender has been made, that our will has at last been brought into complete correspondence with the Divine Will; but each time we find later that a further readjustment is necessary. Time after time it is revealed to us that we are not yet in complete harmony with God. Again and again, we discover that we are not vibrating in sympathy with the eternal music of Divine Love. But if we are willing – and if we will also persevere – then a time must come when our will is entirely at one with the Divine Will, so that we vibrate in perfect correspondence with that which is eternal. In other words, we enter into eternal life, having been reconciled to – or brought into harmony with – God, whom to know is life eternal.

Also, our Lord captivates not only our desires and affections, but also our thoughts. "For where your treasure is, there will your heart be also", and where our heart is, there also will our thoughts be found.

As all our readers know, thought is creative. According to our thoughts, so do we become. As we grow older, the nature of our thoughts is written in our faces. A person of meditation and prayer can be detected at a glance. But greater changes take place within. "As a man thinketh in his heart, so is he". Just as it is true – according to some writers on the subject – that the cultivation of right thinking brings about changes in the cells of the brain, atrophying those which have been used in the past for the purpose of wrong thinking, and bringing into action fresh cells which are used for right thinking, thus making the thinking of right thoughts a habit, so that it is easier to think good thoughts and Godlike thoughts than those that are weak or evil – so also do changes of substance take place within the person who thinks rightly.

What, however, do we mean by thinking rightly? In an elementary way, we mean controlling and guiding the thoughts so that only the highest and best are entertained. It means choosing our thoughts, rejecting those which are either bad or not the highest that we are capable of thinking, and thinking only those thoughts that are the best we know. For instance, instead of allowing thoughts of envy or resentment to occupy the mind, we exert the will so that the mind thinks only thoughts of goodwill, forgiveness and brotherly love. Instead of allowing thoughts of impurity or sensual love to enter the mind, we think instead only of the purity of Heaven and of that greater love that transcends sex, or self, or time and space – and which is eternally self-sacrificing – in fact, the love of Christ. Again, we do not allow thoughts of covetousness or worldly desire to possess our mind. When we are nearly knocked off our feet by the air suction caused by a lordly saloon car, costing thousands of pounds, as it flashes past us, or when we see a lovely mansion gleaming amid miles of beautiful parkland, we do not covet wealth or possession, even though we do not yet possess the spiritual insight which makes us smile at the thought. Instead, we bless the owners and pray for their happiness. This may seem foolish to many, but it is the only way to liberation and freedom from the tyranny of the Prince of this world.

Right thinking, such as we have just briefly and partially described, has been practised by the brave and noble of all ages. When the masses have wanted to give in, the brave few have refused to entertain thoughts of fear and failure. When given opportunities of revenge, they have refused to think of retaliation and have been magnanimous instead.

We find that we are touching the fringe of a vast and wonderful field of exploration.

The outward action is simply the fruit of thought. When our Lord said, "Be ye perfect even as your Father in Heaven is perfect," he meant that our every thought must be pure and lovely and perfect, and not merely that our actions should conform to a certain high standard. At the very springs of our being – the very source – before thoughts can form in us, we have to be cleansed and brought into correspondence with the Divine.

So will we find that right thinking is really prayer, and that prayer and meditation are based upon thought control. Those who have learned how to meditate in the quietude of the presence of God have achieved this through persistent practice of thought selection. Patiently have they put on one side every unwanted thought, and again and again have turned their thought and attention to God.

Brother Lawrence was able to practise the Presence of God simply because he continually turned his thoughts towards God and conversed with Him.

This may all sound very easy. The beginner may say: "The life follows the thoughts, and according to the nature of our thoughts so we become; therefore, I will think only noble, pure, strong, lovely thoughts – in fact, I will think God's thoughts after Him. I will do God's will in my thoughts." He starts, but finds that old habits of thought are too strong for him. But if he perseveres, he will make a certain amount of progress in spite of repeated setbacks. Sooner or later, however, the aspirant will find that they need help, for there are powers and forces working against them which are far greater and cleverer than they. Their prayer for help is heard, however, and they find that the unwanted thoughts – the evil suggestions, the enticements to sin or to think of sin – can be overcome, not in their own strength at all, but by turning to Christ immediately. The power of Christ then works on their behalf so that the temptation is overcome and the thoughts kept pure and, in the highest sense, positive.

The battle of the soul is the battle against wrong thoughts. It is a continual conflict with evil or unworthy thoughts and suggestions. We all know nowadays of the power of suggestion – how a suggestion accepted becomes part of the life. What we are subjected to is suggestion. Evil is suggested to us in the same way that suggestion is given to a subject by a hypnotist. Every time that we look to Christ and rely on the Spirit for help, this power of evil suggestion is broken. This is the only way. Positive thinking without Christ leads the one who practises it to egoism and pride. This again may lead to the greatest error of all – the delusion that they are the Deity, or that they are equal with God. All teaching that tries to make a God out of humanity, without repentance or being changed or born again, is Luciferian. It keeps us forever in outer darkness, and we can never approach the Light until we repent and surrender to God.

Now the effect of doing the will of God, of prayer, meditation, right thinking, and living the life of Christ, in the strength of the Spirit, here on earth, is more than mental. It is something more than a change of thought, of mental attitude, of consciousness. It is nothing less than a change of substance. Eternal life necessitates an eternal body. The spirit cannot function without a body, and the joyous and beautiful aeonian life is only possible to those who possess a spiritual body. The astral body, so the greatest mystics teach, is soon cast aside, and what then?

Our Lord declared that those who believe on Him and follow Him shall not be subject to the second death. This is true, and is possible because those who follow Him possess, or have built up within them, a spiritual body into which death cannot enter. It cannot be assaulted by Lucifer, it cannot be affected by the powers of darkness, death and corruption can have no dominion over it. It is eternal, even as God is eternal. This spiritual body is not self-created, although we have to help in its up-building; it is made out of God's own substance, and because of this it is eternal.

Every time that we look upwards to God, raising our thoughts to heavenly things, desiring only that our will should be in harmony with the Divine Will, every time that we do this, the power of God's Life and His Spirit flow into us, regenerating us and building up our spiritual body. God supplies the power and the substance, but we have to do the looking up.

Regeneration does not mean spiritualising the mortal flesh body; it means building up a body of spiritual flesh and blood. It does not mean that we be translated instead of passing through the change called death. We read that Enoch who walked with God was translated; also that our Lord was, as all who have been perfected, or who have attained immortality can be. Full attainment, however, in this life is, we believe, exceedingly rare. But Swedenborg tells us that those who have partly attained still progress in the afterlife.

The great and important thing is to begin now and make all the progress we can while we are here. Indeed, it is greatly to our own advantage and that of others that we start living the richer, fuller, and more abundant life now.

CHAPTER SEVEN

Living the Universal Life

Before we can live the Universal Life, we must learn to think from the universal standpoint. In other words, we must learn to think as God thinks – broadly, impartially, impersonally, universally – instead of selfishly, narrowly, meanly and personally.

If one is to live the life of the Spirit, one must first of all learn to think after the manner of Spirit – that is, in a godlike way. This entails an entire reversal of thought. Readers often write to say that they cannot agree with this statement or that. Of course they cannot, for they are looking at things from a human standpoint, instead of from the viewpoint of the Spirit (God-Truth).

The way of the Spirit is just the opposite of the way of the flesh, and the viewpoint of God or Truth is the very opposite of that of humanity. Therefore, one who would live the life of the Spirit must first learn to reverse their thinking entirely – by so doing, turning their life completely upside down, so to speak.

The following may, perhaps, help:

> **How Humans Think**
> 1. Personally and selfishly
> 2. In time
> 3. In terms of limitation

> **How God Thinks**
> 1. Impersonally and selflessly
> 2. In eternity
> 3. In terms of limitless freedom

First – Humanity tends to think selfishly. The belief is often that the self is the centre or pivot of the universe, and that everything revolves around one's own experience. The first thought is for self – for "me and mine". A person might give their life for loved ones simply because they are "theirs" – part of "me and mine". No matter what occurs, the first thought is: "How am I going to benefit from this?" or, "Where do I come in?" The dominant life aim becomes to stop others from acquiring what one wants for oneself, and to ensure that oneself and one's immediate circle are comfortably situated. If others apparently have to go short in consequence, it may be a pity – but it is, after all, every person for themselves, and the devil take the hindmost. It has always been so, and always will be – and so on.

By thinking and acting in this way, the individual believes – in their ignorance – that they are benefitting themselves, whereas the reverse is true. The universe is one stupendous whole (God is All in All, i.e., all there is), and in reality, each person is part of that whole. By thinking they are a separate entity or unit – with every person's hand against their own – they separate themselves, in consciousness (though not in reality), from the Whole. In other words, they keep themselves outside the Kingdom of Heaven, or God, through entirely mistaken thinking and a self-centred perspective. That this is not readily apparent is due to the fact that the way of the Spirit is entirely opposite to the wisdom of the senses. It seems that if we think universally and love universally – that is, loving others and all humanity as we love ourselves – we will lose out. Yet this is not so. Apparently, according to sense-wisdom, everything is lost; but in reality, everything is gained, for the person enters the Kingdom of Heaven and begins to live the Universal Life – wherein is perfect freedom, liberty, happiness and peace. The more we extend ourselves outward in love and thought, the more we enter into the fuller, deeper, richer life of the Infinite, the One Whole.

Second – Human beings tend to think from the standpoint of time – whereas God thinks from the standpoint of eternity. It is only natural that people should have a localised outlook, considering that they are passing through time and space (both being merely modes in consciousness) and are subject, more or less, to these limitations. If, however, we are to become free and know the liberty of the Spirit, we must learn to view life – and to think – from the standpoint of eternity. A person who can do this will experience a state of mental calm and poise otherwise impossible to attain. Should they meet with trouble, apparent loss, or injustice – how small it all appears when viewed from the standpoint of eternity or endless being. How paltry temporal ambitions, earthly pomp and power appear in the light of eternity – and how insignificant the loss of these things is seen to be.

Third – People often think in terms of limitation, while Divine Mind thinks in terms of limitless freedom. Humanity is entirely self–limited. But in reality – or in Spirit – being children of God, we are not limited at all. Yet in consciousness we are, because we think we are.

Limitation itself is a limitation of consciousness. There is no limitation in reality – it has no existence apart from our thinking. The universe is mental, and out of the universal mind–stuff (or Spirit substance), we create for ourselves that which corresponds to our thoughts. If our thoughts are thoughts of limitation and lack, we create circumstances that match them. Divine Mind, on the contrary, thinks in terms that are entirely free from limitation of every kind. Knowing the Truth – which is that there is no limit (in reality) of any kind whatever – all Divine thoughts are thoughts of freedom and plenty.

By learning to think universally, we enter into freedom and make possible the living of the deeper, richer life of the Universal.

Chapter Eight

The Problem of Evil

Before we can discuss the problem of evil, it is necessary that we define what evil is.

Firstly, we think of an evil principle, purpose, or power in the universe. Evil, to be truly evil, must be a malevolent power – that is, positive and permanent.

But we ask, "Does such an evil purpose, power, or principle exist in the universe?" The answer is no. If such a principle of evil were a reality, then there would either be two gods of omnipotent power, one warring against the other, or there would be one God who is both good and evil.

Evil, as a power and principle, cannot co-exist with a God who is omnipotent Good. Neither can there be two gods, one warring against the other, because if this were the case, the whole universe would be destroyed. Nor can we conceive of a God who is both good and evil. Therefore, we are forced to the conclusion that there is no evil principle or power in the universe at all.

The student will now ask, "If there is no evil, how do you account for so much evil that is manifested all around us?" Our answer to this is: the evil we see around us is not the evil which we have defined. The evil we see is not due to a malevolent power or principle, and therefore it is not permanent and has no substance in reality. The evil that we come into contact with is something out of which spiritual progress is made.

Nothing out of which good can come can truly be evil. Good has never proceeded from evil yet, and never will do. Good can only come from good, and evil from evil. Therefore, that which we call evil – and which is something from which our highest good is evolved – cannot be evil in actuality and cannot come within our definition of evil.

Without opposition, or the so-called powers of evil, the spiritual unfoldment and development of humanity would be impossible. What is usually regarded as evil is necessary for the production of what we call good. Many people speak lightly of evil and say that pain is evil, that failure is evil, that disease is evil, that illness is evil, that poverty is evil, that bereavement is evil – yet such is very far from being the case. Pain is our best friend, for without it we should destroy or greatly disfigure our bodies. Pain tells us when we are in danger, and it also tells us when we have transgressed the laws of nature. The same applies to sickness and disease, for these tell us when we have transgressed the laws of life. Neither is bereavement evil, for those who have passed through trouble of this kind and have taken it in the right spirit must confess that it has been for their highest good.

It is because the whole universe and the whole of life are based upon Infinite Wisdom and Love – or what we might call Good – that unpleasant circumstances arise in our lives. So far from these being evil, they are the highest possible good. Transgressions of Divine Law come back to us not in the form of punishment, but in the form of remedial experiences and painful circumstances. People ignorantly call these things evil, but they are, in fact, the highest possible good. Sin – whether due to the transgression of law or through failure to live, speak, and act according to truth – always brings sorrow and suffering. Sorrow and suffering are not evil, but are the means by which the soul is turned from the wrong path and directed towards higher and better things.

All who have had much experience of life, and who have learnt its inner meaning, realise that life is not evil, and that there is no principle of evil – although they may meet with very severe temptations. Temptation, although in one sense it may be looked upon as evil, is not evil, according to our definition. Temptation is necessary in order to test us and to develop our character. Without temptation, there could be no progress in the path of attainment. All the powers of darkness are necessary, and all the most subtle temptations to which the soul can be subjected are necessary for spiritual development and growth. Without temptation, it would be impossible to make any progress.

Some readers will say, "Why, then, are we warned to avoid evil, and why did Jesus teach us to pray: deliver us from evil?" This applies to temptation, which we know, by intuition, cannot be given in to without bringing very painful circumstances and darkness and despair of our soul as a natural consequence. We can only resist temptation by turning to God and claiming spiritual strength from our Divine Source. This delivers us from the temptation (from the evil one).

Therefore, those who have had any experience of life, and who understand its inner meaning, realise that there is no evil principle in life, although there may be all sorts of hidden temptations which, if given in to, produce very terrible results. We find that – so far from there being a principle of evil or evil design in life – there is a principle of good that is always seeking to help us. Not, be it noted, to make life easy, but to help in the highest and truest sense. Most of the so-called evil in people's lives is due to their belief that life is evil, and that there is an evil purpose or fate constantly dogging their footsteps. When, however, they realise the truth – that good is the only principle in the universe – they then find that everything works together for good, every time.

A great many people, having realised that there is no evil at work in their individual lives, are yet worried and concerned about the lives of others. They say, "It is not for myself that I am troubled, but the terrible evil that seems to follow some people – apparently innocent – makes me believe that there must be a principle of evil, or a malignant power, at work throughout the universe." This is an entirely erroneous conclusion, for the universe is governed by unchanging law, and what is true of one life is true of every life – past, present, or future. If a law of good operates in one life, then it also operates in all lives. No matter how terrible a person's life may appear to be, it is only Infinite Love and Wisdom, and the Eternal Principle of Good, seeking to get them into the right path.

There are other people who grieve because, while they are willing to admit that there is no evil principle as far as human beings are concerned, yet the sufferings of animals present to them a problem impossible of solution. To such I would say that the same law that applies to humans applies also to animals. The lower orders of creation are evolving and unfolding in much the same way as humanity, and no doubt their various pains, sufferings, and unhappiness are all necessary for their soul growth – for animals have souls just as we do – and without suffering they could not grow.

This must not be used as an excuse for torturing animals, either by vivisection or otherwise. The lower orders of creation are humbler brothers and sisters, and look to us for protection. Humanity sins against these humbler beings, and although Infinite Wisdom is able to work everything together for good, we must bear the responsibility and suffer for our sins in this direction. Our Lord said, "Alas to the world because of offences. It must needs be that offences come; but alas for that man by whom the offence cometh." By this we see that pain and suffering are necessary for the evolution and unfoldment of humankind and creation, yet those who produce the pain and suffering have, in turn, to suffer in the same way. We possess the liberty of choice, and can refrain from attempting to injure others, and when we do this, we cease doing that which produces suffering in our own lives.

Probably the most puzzling thing, to beginners, about Christian teaching is the command not to resist evil. It not only appears hard to do good to those who injure us (apparently), but absolutely foolish also. Yet it is easily understood when we remember that everything that comes to us in life is for our highest good. The source of all things is God (good), who is Infinite Wisdom and Love. Therefore, everything that comes to us in life, no matter how painful the experience may be, is good – that is, love and wisdom in manifestation. We misuse our godlike powers and, instead of our misdeeds and wrong thinking coming back to us in the form of vindictive punishment, they return in the form of remedial experiences. Instead of fighting this apparent evil, all that we need do is to welcome it as a friend, extract from it the good lesson which it has to teach, and then find the love which is behind it all.

Until we are spiritually awakened, we love those who love us or who are kind to us, we do good to those who do good to us – but we hate cordially those who hate us, and return evil for evil, or at any rate, resent being injured or "put upon". When we are ill-treated or wronged, it seems so unjust. We may be robbed of all we possess – it may be the fruits of a lifetime's labours – or we may be slandered or maligned; or we may be discharged from the business which we have laboured to build for others, and find ourselves thrown aside and forgotten; and the injustice of it all bites deeply into our soul. But it is only love and wisdom doing the very best thing for us. There is no evil purpose, really, in it all. At some time, we have made these experiences necessary; therefore, if we rebel against them and resist the apparent evil, we fail to learn their lesson and make other remedial experiences necessary.

All who have had much experience of life know that everything (if we do not oppose it) works together for good. It was because our Lord knew that there is no evil in the disciplines and experiences that come to us, that he was constrained to warn us against resisting evil.

CHAPTER NINE

Reason and Intuition

It is perfectly true that spiritual things cannot be grasped by the intellect, and "realisation" is a condition of knowing in a more searching, inward way. This illumination or knowledge by direct cognition transcends the intellect and reason. For by it we apprehend what the intellect cannot grasp, and human language cannot describe.

Nevertheless, our reason, if used in the right way, is of value in our search for truth.

If we reason wrongly, we not only arrive at erroneous conclusions, but are overwhelmed with perplexity and confusion.

The greatest thinkers admit that before we can reason, we have first to make certain initial assumptions. And this also is necessary in our search for absolute Truth and interior illumination. It depends upon our first premise whether our search is successful or otherwise.

We may base our premise either upon the evidence of the senses, or upon our intuition. If the former, we will find that we are building on a morass – a hopeless confusion. But the latter gives a firm ground and a solid substructure.

We live in a world of illusion. Things are not what they seem. While we are guided by the senses, the greater our knowledge, the more misled and confused we become. Amid this illusion, there is only one sure foundation upon which to build our edifice of logic and reason, and this we reach via intuition. We will thereby arrive at an understanding which will deliver us from perplexity and make us fearless and composed in the face of outward disorder, discord, and apparent calamity.

A simple illustration of the way intuition triumphs over the evidence of the senses is found in the way in which we look upon death. One who sees no farther than the evidence of the senses is quite convinced, if their child dies, that the little one is actually dead, put in a coffin, and buried in the ground. Their grief is the more terrible because of its hopelessness. Another, in similar circumstances, who relies upon intuition rather than sense evidence, knows and believes – although they cannot explain why – that their child is not dead. Grief is assuaged, and by faith, they live their life as though their child were only in the next room or on a visit to friends.

Intuition is, by some, called the religious sense; by others, the voice of God in the soul, or the call of the Higher Self. Without it, humanity would be but as the beasts of the field. With it, we are constantly being drawn back to our Divine Source. Intuition is not the result of either religion or Scripture, for both the latter are the results of the former. The more advanced in unfoldment the soul becomes, the stronger intuition grows, and in all the Scriptures and similar books we find an inner meaning which this inward spiritual faculty tells us is truth.

Without it, the Scriptures are of little value. No matter how much the Truth may glow in the written and inspired word, it can find no echo in the heart unless intuition is present to answer the call.

Intuition declares the truth about God. When I was a child, I was "scared to death" about God and hell, but when I grew older and thought things over more calmly, I felt and knew that God was better than he was painted. Intuition saved me – for apart from it, orthodox teaching would have destroyed my faith.

Intuition tells us that God is the One Supreme Being who is Infinite Love, Justice, Truth, Wisdom, Harmony, Wholeness, Unity, Completeness, and Repose; and it is upon this perfection of God's character that we base our assumptions. Our intuition may be faint and feeble, but somehow, we feel that these things must be true. Starting our reasoning from these assumptions and working outwards, we soon find ourselves in sharp conflict with the evidence of the senses.

God is Love, we say, but soon we find every possible external evidence that God is not love. As the unillumined or unthinking say, "How can God be a God of love, and allow such terrible things to happen?" What can human wisdom say in answer to such a question? Nothing, except to say that there cannot be any such being as a God of Love.

Again, we state, God is Infinite Justice, and then we are confronted with every possible form of apparent injustice. What can human wisdom say to this, except that it is quite evident that there can be no God of Justice?

Yet again, we declare that God is a God of Wholeness, yet all around us we find disease, sickness, ill health, and suffering of every kind. What can human wisdom say to this, except that there can be no God of Wholeness and Health?

What, then, are we to say and do when confronted by sense evidence that is in direct conflict with what we have stated to be the truth, and which intuition tells us must be the truth? Intuition, not having been developed, may be very faint indeed, while the evidence of the senses is so strong and clear that matter–of–fact people smile at us to think that we should ever question it.

Which are we to do? Are we to have faith in our intuition, which is so faint and feeble (apparently), or in the evidence of the senses, which is so obvious and strong?

It is just here that abstract reasoning is most valuable.

If we argue from appearances, we soon reach a state of absolute pessimism and hopelessness. If, however, we argue from our assumptions, based upon our intuition, we reach certain conclusions which are clear–cut, and which become a rock that will support us in the dark hours which come, at some time, to every soul.

We start our reasoning from God, because both intuition and reason tell us that there is one First Cause or central fount from which everything flows. We may proceed as follows:

First Stage

- ***God is***

- ***God is One*** (There can be only one omnipotent being. If there were more, that being would not be omnipotent.)

    Consequently:

- ***God is the author of all that is***
  Therefore, as there is only One Source or Substance:

- ***God is all there is, or all in all***

Second Stage

- ***God is love, and God is all***
  Therefore: **all is love**

- ***God is good, God is all***
  Therefore: **all is good**

- ***God is absolute justice, God is all***

Therefore: **all is justice**

- ***God is absolute wholeness, God is all***
  Therefore: **all is perfectly whole**

- ***God is absolute wisdom, God is all***
  Therefore: **life is an expression of perfect wisdom**

It follows, then, that because ***all is love, all is good, all is justice, all is wholeness, all is wisdom,*** and so on, that none of the experiences of life can be evil, but can only be a perfect manifestation of love and wisdom.

What is required, therefore, is a clearer understanding of truth.

The next thing is to apply the truth. In the face of 'sense evidence' of evil, we take our stand upon the rock of absolute truth, establishing ourselves in it and affirming it. We refuse to be terrorised or intimidated by error, and affirm truth, although apparently, we have the whole sense–world against us. We refuse to admit any other principle than the one principle of good or wholeness, which is always expressed in love and wisdom.

We do not attempt to inflict our will upon life or assert that someone is well who is obviously ill, or that so–and–so is going to do something for us, or that such–and–such a thing will happen in our affairs. This is mainly working with the human mind and can only result in disappointment. Instead of all this joyless effort, we simply turn to the truth of being, and affirm it, and realise it, after which we let the spirit manifest truth outwardly, which it will do according to our faith, clearness of realisation or spiritual vision. We affirm the truth of being, and not the desire of self, that infinite wisdom may manifest in its own way. We do not know what will be manifested, but we do know that whatever it is, it must be good. The form which it takes does not concern us, but we know that the outcome of our faith and declaration of truth will be the highest manifestation of wisdom and love that our present state of unfoldment will allow.

Divine perfection is a present fact. We do not have to alter God's universe, neither do we have to remind the supreme being that He has forgotten us; all that is needed is for us to realise and understand the truth of being more. It is our consciousness that has to be healed, and truth alone can do this.

With what result? Principally this: that it unites us to God and establishes us in truth. The more often we turn to God, the more easily and perfectly can *love* rule our heart and conduct. To the extent that we become changed within will our outward life become transformed, and the cause of the hell which we formerly experienced correspondingly removed.

Hell on earth is caused by ignorance of truth, with its consequent outcome of wrong thinking and action. Through ignorance, we work against the laws of our being.

The purpose of affirming or making statements of truth is not to scare evil away by the magic use of words, but simply to clear away the fog of error, that with the eyes of the soul we may more clearly see that which has always been present – the truth. When truth is realised, the soul is flooded with light and understanding; it knows that which transcends the human mind and which the intellect cannot grasp.

Making use of statements of truth is not done in order to drug the mind or to produce a false belief. Realisation is true spiritual illumination and is not the result of mental drugging. It may be possible to drug the mind by repeating statements of error, but this would have a destructive effect on the life, whereas the use of statements of truth has a constructive and transforming effect.

It is impossible for anyone consciously to follow the teaching of this lesson for a few years and not to become changed, both in character and life. "The proof of the pudding is in the eating." This proof is being demonstrated by thousands today. Those who base their beliefs in a God who is *one* – who is infinite love, wisdom, wholeness and perfection – and who trust the infinite mind instead of finite understanding, being willing to be led by the spirit, are having proved to them again and again that they are on the right path.

Those who live in the consciousness of the allness of good enter a fuller and richer life. They have no cause to worry and nothing to fear. Theirs is a carefree life of utter dependence on the one source which can never fail.

To recapitulate:

1. First, we make certain assumptions based upon intuition.

2. Secondly, by abstract reasoning, we arrive at certain conclusions from which we form statements of truth.

3. Thirdly, we establish ourselves in truth and continue to repeat and declare the truth and live in its light and power.

4. Fourthly, realisation of truth comes to the soul in a sense of conviction and certainty – after which truth manifests in the life, charms away its discords, heals our diseases, supplies our needs, and brings peace to our souls.

Chapter Ten

Divine Plenty

There must be no attempt to misuse spiritual powers in order to obtain wealth, or even daily bread and the simplest necessities of life. When the student begins to realise their higher spiritual and mental powers, they are sorely tempted to misuse them. What was true of our Lord is equally true, in a smaller way, of us. "Command that these stones be made bread," said the tempter or tester of souls. But our Lord refused to do so, although he was very hungry. Why? Because it is a spiritual law that the higher powers of the personality or lower ego must not be misused to produce phenomena for the gratification of desire, no matter how innocent a character it might be.

Some readers may demur at this point, and say that Jesus turned water into wine, and fed the five thousand in this way. But I very much doubt it. I find no evidence that these miracles were performed by the personality. It is not recorded that Jesus, as a human, commanded the water to magically change into wine, nor do we read of him commanding the bread and fishes to be multiplied. Coming nearer to our own times, we do not find Dr.

Muller commanding food to appear on his orphan boys' tables or indulging in some magical practice. No, the miracles of Jesus and the wonderful answers to prayers which Dr. Muller experienced were accomplished by looking to the Father and trusting him entirely, in absolute and utter faith, to meet the needs of the moment.

Jesus was tempted to command the stones to be made bread, and he refused. When he fed the five thousand, he lifted up his eyes and blessed, etc. No two methods could be more dissimilar.

In the case where water was turned into wine, recorded in St John's Gospel, there is to be found no commanding of such a transformation to be made. There was simply a calm expectation that the need would be met by the Spirit.

It has been said by some advanced teachers that the difference between commanding stones to be made bread and the feeding of the five thousand was merely that whereas the former would have been done to appease the hunger of Jesus, the latter was for the sake of the multitude. They argue that while it is wrong to overrule the forces of nature for one's own benefit, it is quite permissible to do so for the sake of others. This cannot be the case. It is the principle involved that counts, not merely its application.

Humans, when they reach a certain stage of understanding, are capable of exercising occult powers over the forces of nature. It is then that they are tested by being tempted to misuse their occult powers. It is possible to produce wealth magically, but it is a crime to do so, and foolish also, because those who misuse their powers in this way come down to misery and want. No matter what it may be, that which is magically produced cannot endure. It is false creation, and therefore has no reality, true substance or permanence. In addition, riches produced magically bring with them misery and unhappiness beyond description. The unhappy devotee is caught up and dashed about by forces which they have set in motion, but which are quite beyond their power to control.

The reader may say at this point, "Is there then no higher law of supply? Is there no provision for God's children except through the sweat of the brow and by labour, toil, or successful competitive business or professional service?" Yes, there is, as anyone who studies the Gospels must admit, but it is the very antithesis of "commanding these stones that they be made bread". It is possible to those who are prepared to follow the Spirit utterly and entirely, who, while not neglecting their business or calling, place, day by day, their full trust and reliance upon God for all their needs.

Henry Victor Morgan, in one of his wise articles, writes that he suffered lack and restriction until he met a person who lived, fully, the life of the Spirit. This person had not a dollar to their name, yet they possessed the riches which can never fade away. They knew that they could never lack any necessary thing, because the Spirit was looking after them.

The majority of Truth students have the opportunity of working either in a business or in some profession, and many very wisely make their affairs a subject for prayer, that they may be divinely blessed and guided in all that they undertake. But there are those who, for certain reasons, cannot engage in remunerative employment. Likewise, there come times in the lives of most people, when ordinary sources of supply fail or dry up, when unless they can entirely rely upon the Spirit for supply, great is their alarm and distress.

The highest life is one of faith, of entire dependence upon God for all that we need. And this is to rely no longer upon wealth, or riches, or possessions, but simply upon God, who is the one spiritual source of all that is.

Such faith is rare, yet Dr. Muller demonstrated it. Never once were his orphan boys without food, although, more than once, it was not at hand apparently, when the boys were told to sit down for their meal. But at the right moment, it duly came. Never once did the supply fail.

Dr. Muller had great faith, and it was never betrayed, though it was tested over and over again. And, in that it never faltered, the supply never failed.

It is not easy to give up clinging to money, wealth, or material sources of supply; to cease holding and relying upon the things of the world to keep us from want. But if we would tread the path of liberation, we must attempt it. In small things first, and then in greater, we can learn to trust the Spirit instead of the flesh – God instead of mammon.

As, more and more, we depend upon God, gradually we learn to live the life of the Spirit.

The Truth demands that we rely wholly upon our Divine Source, and not upon others, whether relatives or otherwise. There is a tremendous difference between letting ourselves drift and living a life of faith. There should also always be a strong desire to work. St. Paul worked as a sail-maker at times, but when he travelled as an evangelist, other people supplied his needs. In each case, the supply came from God; in each case, he did, thoroughly, the work that came to hand.

The teaching of Christ with regard to supply is that what is necessary for our perfect expression comes to us if we will only leave off worrying, straining, and fearing – and if we will only trust the Higher Spiritual Being, or Self, or Father in Heaven, completely and fully. This does not mean that we should become careless and let things drift; but neither does it mean that we are to struggle, fight, grab, pinch, hoard, scrape, or seek after riches. What it does mean is that we are to get on with the business of life, to devote our attention to work and service – not for what they bring to us in the way of money, but for their own sake. If our principal aim is to improve the quality of our work and service, God, or life, or principle, will look after the supply.

There is hardly anyone who cannot do work of some kind. The very blind, such as the men of St. Dunstan's, teach us that. If we do not work when we can, we become as parasites, receiving but not giving.

If we are out of work, some sort of service should be undertaken during hours not spent in seeking employment. Work should be sought, however, with a firm belief that life does not want us to be idle – that there is just the position we need waiting for us, and that the Spirit is leading us to it – a position in which we can serve our fellows in love. Life is always trying to promote us to something better, if we will only be led by the Spirit and will qualify ourselves by increased capacity, worth, and efficiency, for larger and more responsible service.

Let us, however, clearly state that whereas the natural person must fulfil the law of the lower plane – that "if they will not work, neither shall they eat" (in some way, suffering will ensue) – and whereas all people must obey the law of co-operative service, spiritual people, truly, are not dependent upon work for supply. They work, often very hard indeed, in order to serve, but not for food or clothing, money or reward of any kind. They look to God, life, or principle for supply – or rather, they trust God implicitly, either through faith or through knowledge – and their wants are always supplied: not oversupplied, but just enough.

If one were to expect to become rich, in a worldly sense, by this means, they would be disappointed. If they thought that because they looked to the Infinite Supply, they would magically find themselves loaded with thousands of pounds, they would find that they were mistaken. We are not told that the prodigal child, after returning to their parent, went about with half the fatted calf under one arm and a big loaf of bread under the other, for fear they might run short of food. Spiritual people, finding themselves in their Father's House, where there is always plenty, 'travel light'.

They are encumbered with no superfluous possessions. They have no investments to worry them, but every day their wants are supplied. They may be poor from a worldly-wise standpoint, but rich from a spiritual standpoint. Possessing the riches which fade not away, how foolish they would be to want more than enough of this world's goods!

But it must also be pointed out that we can restrict ourselves seriously by our thoughts. If we think that our supply depends upon others, or the state of trade, or upon the precarious earnings of another, and that if these fail, we are done for, we not only become the victims of worry and care, but we also subject ourselves to the limitations which we recognise.

If we doubt that God can supply our needs when trade is bad, or we are out of work, we limit ourselves and prevent our supply from manifesting. Or if we think that evil tends toward us, or that poverty is dogging our steps, again we limit ourselves and keep our good away from us.

Further, if we think that God is indifferent, approving of poverty and misery – especially if we think that God almost takes pleasure in that – we thereby limit our circumstances and open the door to privation and want.

But if we believe that God is good, and that God is omnipotent and able to supply us no matter what may happen, all that we need is bound to manifest from somewhere, just at the right time.

And, if we believe that God is an abundant God, who thinks and creates on a liberal and generous scale, who can only see us plentifully and bountifully provided for – bountiful and adequate supply will surely find us.

Again, if we believe and affirm that good only is seeking us, and if we expect it to manifest and confidently look for it with faith and confidence, all necessary supply is sure to appear.

What we have to do is:

– To think well of our Heavenly Father.
– To expect great things from Him.
– To think from the standpoint of unfailing divine bounty.
– To praise God continually for His divine love and abundant blessings.

Each night and morning, time should be spent in thanking our Heavenly Father for the many blessings of life, and in realising, in the quiet of our souls, that God is the perfect supply of all humankind. This should be done without fear, anxiety, worry or strain. "In quietness and confidence shall be your strength."

Then, during the day, all suggestions of want, or impending poverty, or financial care, should be met by statements of truth.

Many people, when thoughts or suggestions of poverty or financial trouble come to them, merely dismiss them. This is not sufficient. It is far better than brooding over them, but it does not conquer the difficulty. Each suggestion of lack must be overcome by truth.

In the old days, when I was often in great financial difficulty, I used to try to find relief from worry by seeking amusement. It is true that while the entertainment was on, it was possible to forget the care, or partly so, but as soon as the performance was over, the trouble and worry came back again as badly as ever. Forgetting our troubles for a time does not help – inwardly, the suggestion continues its work, and outwardly, it is reflected in the form of growing difficulty and trouble.

Psychologists tell us that what is accepted by the unconscious mind as an autosuggestion appears in the external life as an actual fact of experience. Therefore, what we have to do is defeat the suggestions of lack and want, and replace them with truth. If truth is accepted by the inner mind in place of suggestions of error or evil, then truth – wholeness, perfection – is manifested in the outer life as fact and experience.

Therefore, we have to overcome all suggestions of lack and limitation; all suggestions that God is not able to supply our needs, or that God is not willing to do so; all suggestions that circumstances are controlling us; all suggestions of fear; all suggestions that we are separated from our divine source and are not one with the infinite love, wisdom, life, wholeness, and power.

These suggestions of evil can be overcome only by truth. By affirming our oneness with our source, we cut the ground from under all suggestions of evil. We can use a short sentence, or statements of truth, that convey to our mind all that is necessary. Any statement that links us up to our divine source and creates in the mind a sense of oneness, fellowship, trust, love, union, and so on, is all-powerful — simply because it is truth — while every suggestion of evil is error and possesses no reality.

What we have, then, to do is to believe that the divine source of all is both able and willing to supply all our needs; that we are one with that source, and therefore, all things are ours; that nothing can separate us from the love of God.

Also, we have to meet every suggestion of evil with an affirmative truth, repeating some simple, inclusive sentence until the suggestion of lack is overcome and destroyed.

From the above, it will now be realised that we do not have to misuse our higher powers by "commanding these stones that they be made bread", but simply to cleanse all error from the mind so that the light of truth may illumine our understanding and reflect itself in our outward life and circumstances.

CHAPTER ELEVEN

Supply Consciousness

It is not easy to apprehend the truth of this matter. We have to distinguish between **commanding** (or compelling) the invisible forces to act for us and **allowing** (or letting) the Spirit (or our Father in Heaven) to supply us with all that we need. The temptation to misuse the power of the Spirit comes to all of us as we reach a certain level of spiritual development. The soul, there and then, makes the discovery that it is possessed of a wonderful power.

What shall we do with this power? Shall we misuse it for the sake of satisfying our bodily hunger, or acquiring a few of the baubles of life? Or shall we use the power rightly – in better living and higher service? Like our Lord, we have to go into the wilderness to be tempted. Shall we take the right hand or the left? We can go on inwardly developing – for, having reached a certain point, it is not possible to stand still. But one path leads to spiritual perversion. We may so affiliate with the dark brethren – even attain thereby to fourth-dimensional powers – yet whose will is evil. Or, by taking the right path, we may follow Christ and reach that glorious state declared by St John:

> "Beloved, now are we the sons of God; and it does not yet appear what we shall be, but we know that when He shall appear, we shall be like Him."
>
> 1 John 3:2

At this point, we must declare where we are – which path we will choose – receiving thereby the seal of Christ, or what is referred to as "the mark of the beast".

The latter implies the occult misuse of spiritual powers. If, however, we follow our Lord's teaching and put it into practice, we shall "bear his seal in our foreheads". When he comes, he will know us by reason of that seal, and we will know him, intuitively, through the Spirit within us.

To visualise wealth or money and to will it into manifestation is malpractice. It is the first step in black magic. It is equivalent to commanding stones to be made bread. The temptation is a severe one to those who know something of occult powers. By visualising and willing – by dominating and commanding – one may achieve quite magical results, if they have reached this stage of power. But if they follow the Christ way of depending entirely upon the One who is willing to guide us, putting ourselves in divine hands, very different will be the experience. We may have to remain a long while in the wilderness – amid apparent lack and limitation –

tempted by doubts and fears; but we will win through, if we are true and steadfast, after which we can never really lack again.

The attainment of the *supply consciousness* marks a great step forward in spiritual experience. I believe that, in the lives of many of us, a time is coming when we shall be severely tested upon this very point. Not only in this, but in many other things, the choice will have to be made between the true Christ way and the dark ways of magic and mental malpractice. The ordinary means of life may fail – then we shall have to look entirely to interior means for supply. If we have not learned the Christ way, the way of black magic will appear to be the only apparent alternative.

The Christ way is not, however, one of drift and carelessness. It does not mean that we have to leave off working profitably. As a rule, except in the case of those who become teachers of Truth and voluntarily choose a life of comparative poverty, making God's service their single aim, the work at which we can earn the most money is oftentimes the occupation for which we are most suited, and in which we can be most helpful to the community.

There are striking exceptions, however. If we follow Christ's teaching, it does not mean that we are to let things drift, in the "hope" that accounts will be met, and that the wherewithal to meet life's necessities will find itself, so to speak. Indeed, it is very different. Christ's way demands the exercise of a very lively, vigorous and strong faith in God as our Divine Supply. Paradoxically, the life of trust and rest in God is the most strenuous of all. Nothing develops soul character more. No life is so vigorous as that of quiet trust in God. Each one who tries to live such a life is tested again and again, until either they become frightened and give up the quest, or they overcome and live ever afterwards the life of faith and utter dependence upon God.

The way to the Christ consciousness of everlasting supply is by prayer. Prayer, to be of any use, must be something more than the repetition of beautiful sentences which may not touch our souls. It must also be something different from begging God to give us something. The highest form of prayer is, of course, communion with God in the quietness of the soul – just feeding upon Him who is the Bread of Life.

Most readers, probably, are not advanced enough for this. They need something simpler and more definite. This is a human weakness, but, as we are all more or less subject to such human weaknesses, it must be allowed for. The average seeker after Truth is worldly and practical enough to want something that will "cut ice". They are in trouble of some sort and want God to get them out of it. Very elementary, you say – but how human!

How shall they pray, then? Shall they supplicate? No, for to do so would impress a sense of limitation still more deeply upon the mind. Our Lord said: "And all things whatsoever ye shall ask in prayer, believing, ye shall receive" (Matthew 21:22).

Again, in Mark 11:22–25, we have the following vital instructions as to how we should pray in order to receive (i.e. manifest outwardly that which is already ours in Spirit): "And Jesus said unto them, 'have faith in God'".

> "Verily, I say unto you, whosoever shall say unto this mountain, Be thou taken up and cast into the sea; and shall not doubt in his heart, but shall believe that what he saith cometh to pass; he shall have it.

> "Therefore, I say unto you, All things whatsoever ye pray and ask for, believe ye have already received them, and ye shall have them".
>
> KJV Revised Version

Again, in Philippians iv, 6, we are told:

> "In nothing be anxious, but in everything by prayer and supplication with thanksgiving let your requests be made known to God".

Therefore, in order to pray aright, we have to give thanks for those things which are already ours in Spirit, although they may not yet be manifest outwardly.

Many lives are barren, restricted and miserable simply because no thanksgiving is offered to God for visible blessings – to say nothing of those blessings already bestowed but not yet in manifestation.

In praying to God, who is the supreme source of everything there is, we must realise and acknowledge that God is the **only** source of supply. All material channels belong only to the surface of things. They are not manifestations of Divine Supply, but merely evidences of finite limitation. The more we look to material sources, the more restricted our lives become, and the more closely bound we are by human limitations.

While people are bound by human limitations – such as conditions of employment, state of trade, position of the money market, the letting or selling of property, and the like – God, or Spirit, is not in any way limited by these restrictions. In Spirit, there is no limitation whatever. Spirit, or God, cannot be restricted or affected by bad trade or by any limitation of which we can conceive. Spirit is perfectly free, all-powerful, and quite capable of dealing with any difficulty.

We may be in want today, with our circumstances such that no deliverance seems possible – when to human sense and wisdom, the outlook is hopeless. Yet the situation presents no difficulty whatever to Spirit, or God, who is omniscient and can triumph over every difficulty and situation.

Some of you doubtless keep chickens. If so, you have often been amused – if not exasperated – because when one chicken has got outside the run, and you open the door for it, it yet cannot find its way back. It keeps wandering to and fro, trying vainly to find a way through the wire netting – getting fairly excited because it cannot do so – yet all the time the door is open for it, but it cannot appreciate the fact. The task of getting back to the run presents an insuperable difficulty to the hen because its mind is so limited it cannot understand that the open door is for it to pass through. You, on the contrary, see no difficulty in the problem at all, because your mind is free of the limitations which restrict the mind of the hen.

In the same way, while problems appear to us to be beyond solution, the Infinite Mind of God can experience no difficulty under any circumstances whatever. Therefore, no matter how hopeless or difficult our circumstances may appear to us to be, they can present no difficulty to Infinite Mind. It is just as easy for God – or Spirit, or Infinite Mind – to deliver us when outwardly everything seems lost and hopeless as it is for God to keep us when times are good, and no one but a lazy person could help earning a good living. There is absolutely no difference to Infinite Mind, simply because there can never be any problem presented to a mind that is infinite and to which everything is always perfectly easy. It is only a finite mind – one that thinks in pairs of opposites – that can meet with difficulties or problems.

Therefore, it follows that in order to solve all our problems regarding supply, we have only to bring them to God, or Spirit, for they can present no difficulty to Infinite Mind. If we bring our financial problems to God, having done all we can to solve them by ordinary legitimate means, they must disappear – for there is no problem from God's side; it only exists on our side, and is due to the finiteness of our human mind.

If we bring the problem of supply to God, allowing God to raise it out of the finite limitations which are the cause of the problem, Infinite Wisdom quickly reveals to us a way of escape. It is revealed to us where we have gone wrong, and in what way we have worked against Divine Law, thus raising a barrier to our own progress. A way of escape is provided, which should be made use of with a grateful heart. The lesson which the experience has brought us should be stored up in the heart and memory, so that we walk more wisely in future.

Not only is there no problem on the divine side – for Infinite Mind can never be presented with any difficulty – but Spirit, or God, is also the only source of material supply, in the same way that God is the source of all life and power. God, or Infinite Spirit, is not only the source of all things spiritual, but also of all things material.

Christ is not only the bread from heaven – the spiritual, life-giving food for every soul who will become as a little child and enter the Kingdom – but also the one source of all material supply. Christ is the one substance, or **that** from which all substance springs.

The great secret of successful prayer is to recognise that God is not only the one source of all we need, but that there is no supply except that which comes from this one central fount.

As soon as the beginner tries to think of God as their only source of supply, they quickly realise that their mind has been revolving around an entirely different idea. The weakest think: *If only someone would help me, I would be all right. If only some rich relative, or someone who has more than they know what to do with, might take pity on me or take a fancy to me!*

Others think: *If only I had a balance at the bank, I should feel safe!* (By all means, have your bank balance, if you can – but do not rely upon it instead of upon God.)

Others think: *If only trade were better, or if I were a better salesperson, or if there were a chance of promotion in my office, or if such-and-such schemes were successful,* and so on.

What we all have to do is to get our minds away from material channels and human limitations, and instead concentrate them upon God as the one source of all our spiritual and material supplies.

What is needed is for a new centre to be formed in the mind, around which thoughts – both unconscious and conscious – shall revolve. In the ordinary way, thoughts revolve around a fixed idea of human limitation and restriction. This brings lack and want into the external life.

What is needed is for the centre, or fixed idea, to be born again of the Spirit, so that the thoughts revolve around the idea of divine, inexhaustible plenty, instead of that of human lack and limitation.

We can bring the truth home to ourselves and our consciousness by saying:

> God is my supply.
> God is my only supply.
> There is no supply apart from God.

Then one can use an affirmation such as the following:

> I look to God alone for my supply, and God supplies
> me out of infinite riches.

If a statement such as this is taken into the Silence night and morning, and allowed to sink deeply into our mind and heart until there is an answering response, a new and richer consciousness will be built up – and it will reflect in the external life in the form of greater abundance.

It matters not how hopeless our circumstances may be – they will become fluidic if we take our problem into the Divine Presence (the Silent Place of the Infinite) in this manner. The poor pastor may think their life cramped and limited by a meagre stipend, the struggling writer by the harsh conditions governing obscure authorship, the underpaid music teacher by poverty–stricken rates of payment. But all things are possible with God, whose mind is infinite in all directions.

God, or Spirit, is the one substance. Spirit is God in manifestation. What we term matter is spiritual substance cognised within the limits of a three-dimensional consciousness. Everything, truly, is Spirit – or formed out of spiritual substance. Because of this, by looking to the Spirit for all supply, we reach the source and beginning of all things.

We realise then that, because we are spiritual beings – at one with the One Spirit, living and moving and having our being in Spirit – all our wants are supplied in Spirit, and that sooner or later this truth must be reflected into human consciousness in the form of greater material supply. Such supply will almost always come through human channels, but it will come nonetheless from our Divine Spiritual Source. Things will happen in such surprising ways, sometimes, as will convince us that we are dealing with spiritual law – not mere luck, chance, or fortuitous circumstances.

Jesus Christ realised the spiritual source of all material things. Indeed, He did this so clearly that, as He gave thanks, the fishes and loaves were multiplied a thousandfold. Let us also look into the fathomless Spirit around us, and give thanks to God in the same manner – with absolute faith and conviction – then great things will manifest themselves.

Chapter Twelve

Health

Think from the standpoint that because you are one with the Infinite Life, therefore you are perfectly whole, in body and in mind. Only health, strength, wholeness and physical and mental well-being can manifest in your life and body, if you think and live with this Truth-thought predominant in your mind.

> The Power of Thought (old edition)

Just as God is the only source of supply – for all things and all substance come from one spiritual Source – so also God is the only source of health. There is no life apart from God. God is life as well as love, and this life is, of course, infinite. It can never be limited in reality. It can never become weak, or diseased, or imperfect. It remains perfect always.

God's life, however, can be limited in our consciousness – although not in reality. We can imperfectly apprehend the perfection of God's life, due to the fact that we have fallen (in consciousness) from the Divine Idea. It is our apprehension that is imperfect. Because a scholar does not rightly apprehend the laws of mathematics, and consequently is wrong in their calculations, it does not prove that these laws are imperfect. It simply proves that the scholar has failed to grasp certain principles that are inherently – and indeed eternally – true.

As God's life is perfect, it follows that the life of humanity must be inherently perfect also. Why, then, is this interior wholeness and perfection not more generally manifest?

That it is not so is due to several reasons. One is that many people eat twice or thrice the quantity of food that is necessary. Overeating kills more surely than alcohol. Another reason is that people are not content to eat things as nearly as possible in their natural state but must devitalise them by refining them.

Many also – of a delicate, highly-strung type, living a sedentary life – feed upon a diet more suitable for a hunter or farm labourer. On the other hand, there are those who worry themselves into ill health through food faddism. Every morsel they eat becomes a source of anxiety. If they cannot get their special food, specially prepared, they become ill – not because of the change of food, but because of the fear-thoughts and anxieties which obsess them. Again, there are those who take no exercise. One wonders how some people are able to live at all, as we watch them waddling from a tea shop (after having taken an unnecessary and therefore harmful meal) to their motor cars. The poor need never sigh for the luxuries of the well-to-do – for with them, all too frequently, come ill health and surgical operations.

But these things are as nothing compared with hidden, fundamental causes. In fact, they are but the offspring – even as the herding of huge masses of people into cities, where they live twilight lives in fog, noise, smoke and ugliness, travelling in tubes and working in sunless offices – is a result of a wrong attitude of mind and soul. It is selfishness, greed, and love of ease and luxury that have brought our big cities into being, and it is only the Christ–love and unselfishness that can dissolve them and bring the people to a saner and more natural mode of living.

The fundamental causes of ill health are mental, spiritual, and emotional. Our mortal imagination falls short of the Divine Imagination and creates, or produces, disease and imperfection in place of Divine Perfection. The life power is good, but through being diverted into wrong channels it produces what we call evil.

The imagination is a matrix or mould, which shapes the outward life out of the Life Force. The Life Force is never evil, but it becomes moulded into the wrong pattern. In a foundry, the same molten metal can be poured either into a perfect or an imperfect mould. From the former, we get a perfect casting, but from the latter, an imperfect one. The metal is the same in each case, and in both moulds it flows into every corner, doing its work perfectly. But because one mould is imperfect, an imperfect casting is produced from the self-same metal which, in a correct mould, produces a correct casting. Therefore, our imagination must be changed if the perfect Life of God is to find expression in our bodies, after the Divine Pattern.

This we cannot do of ourselves. We do not know what the Divine Pattern is. Therefore, we have to be born again, after the Spirit, and to be changed inwardly into the Divine Likeness.

This, however, becomes possible, even as we wholeheartedly seek after God, and meditate upon His Wholeness and Perfection, in the *quiet place* (the Silence), realising our oneness with Him, through Christ. Christ then becomes our healer.

> "In the same way, the Spirit also helps us in our weakness; for we do not know what prayers to offer, nor in what way to offer them. But the Spirit himself pleads for us with yearnings that can find no words, and the Searcher of hearts knows what the Spirit's meaning is, because his intercessions for God's people are in harmony with God's will."
> – Romans 8:26 (Weymouth's translation)

When, therefore, we rest in the *quiet place*, even though we can formulate no prayer, the Spirit helps us, and, as it were, prays for us in the only right way. Of ourselves, we might pray for that which is not in harmony with God's will, but the Spirit prays for us according to the Divine Will, which is wisdom and love.

What we have to do, then, is to rest in God's Presence, and to commune in the Spirit. For this is the truest form of prayer, and it always brings to us that which is for our highest good.

The Life of God is perfect. It is the very essence of perfection, wholeness and power. Complete and harmonious, it lacks nothing, neither does it contain any possible disorder. By opening ourselves, by an act of surrender, to the Divine inflow, we become filled with God's perfect life and power. By doing this, we become attuned to the Divine and Infinite on all planes of being. The perfect harmony thus produced between spirit, soul and body is expressed in the form of constant health and well-being.

The more we raise our thoughts above the depressing things of material sense with its imperfections and disharmonies, the nearer we approach the Divine Ideal and become at one with our Spiritual Source. The disorder that we experience outwardly, or through the senses, is the result of thought, for everything in form is the result of thought. Then, of whose thought is disease or ill health the result? Surely not God, for His thoughts are perfect, and can only produce that which is perfect. No – disease and disorder are not the result of God's thought, but of a corrupt mortal imagination, which perverts the whole current of human thought, causing us to think perpetually, both consciously and unconsciously, around a pessimistic idea of disease, weakness, misery and death. There may be conflict, repression, reversed suggestion, and so on, but these are all forms of disorder due to lack of harmony with the Divine Idea of perfection and order.

Realisation is reached through meditation upon absolute Truth, by stating the Truth, and by arguing oneself out of mortal error, until one understands absolute Truth in the soul, apprehending it through spiritual revelation or illumination, or intuition, instead of through the intellect. In other words, realisation is the result of scientific prayer.

All that has to be done is to cast out human error and let in the light of God's eternal Truth. When this takes place, the subconscious not only accepts the Truth, but harmony is restored through the whole being: conflict ceases, repressions are dissolved, complexes are exploded, and rest and peace pervade the whole system.

In spite of the undoubted success of certain psychological methods of healing, we still maintain – and wholeheartedly believe – that the true healing of all ailments of mind and body is to be found in real prayer.

Many who are trying in vain to master their thoughts and to think along positive lines would be successful if they cultivated the habit of true prayer. They realise that if they are to be well, they must change their habit of thought – but they find it difficult, if not impossible, to do so. They cannot control their conscious thoughts, to say nothing of their subconscious thinking; therefore, their unsatisfactory state of health continues, and every department of life suffers also. They know that if they are to be well, they must leave off thinking thoughts of weakness, depression, grief, worry, care, fear, resentment, impurity and lust – as well as refraining from dwelling upon sickness generally, and their own ailments in particular – but they find that to do so is very difficult. Some give it up and say: "It can't be done." "How," they claim, "can I refrain from worrying when I'm worried to death? Or how can I refrain from fear when I'm sick with fear? It is utterly impossible in my circumstances. If my environment were different, or if my health were better, I could perhaps think rightly; but as things are, it is impossible. I should like to see one of these complacent teachers placed in my shoes. What would their thoughts be like if they felt as ill as I do sometimes?"

Let it be said here that if such people had their circumstances altered, it would not help them to think rightly. They would leave off trying at once. Their present painful circumstances are the best thing possible for them, for they drive or compel them to try to think correctly.

Better, however, to try to think rightly and fail than never to try at all. Failure compels us all to find out why we have failed and to seek a remedy.

And we find it in true prayer – which indeed is the great "thought changer".

What is true prayer?

It is getting into touch with our Divine Source. It is our retirement from all that is external, to the *secret place*, there to meditate upon God and to commune with Him. Every time we meditate upon God in this way, and realise our oneness with Him, we to that degree undergo a change, into His likeness. Every time that we retire from the world of the senses to commune with our spiritual Source, a centre or point in us becomes shifted, tending ever nearer to the Divine Centre.

Our thoughts revolve around their centre. If the dominant note in us is God and Perfection, our thoughts will revolve around it and be of this character. But if it is the feeling of separateness, weakness, fear, disease, etc., then our thoughts will be like unto this, in spite of our efforts to control them. But daily meditation in the secret place of the soul upon God and His divine character will change the very fountain of our thoughts.

By daily communion with God as our Source and Centre, and by recalling the Truth of our oneness with Him to our remembrance frequently during the day by the use of statements of Truth – so guarding our thoughts – we become established in God's Eternal Life, Wholeness and Power.

> I open myself to the inner, renewing, healing of the Spirit.

CHAPTER THIRTEEN

Wholeness

Health is harmony – a delicate balance and adjustment between spirit, soul, mind and body. This harmony is dependent entirely upon the greater harmony between ourselves and God. So long as there is a conflict of will; so long as there is hate or resentment; so long as there is selfishness, or while there is fear, this harmony cannot exist. Therefore, the bedrock cause of health is spiritual harmony, all healing being a restoration of harmony between man and his Divine Source.

Within You is the Power, by H.T. Hamblin, 1921

We are brought back to the fundamental truth underlying all religious teaching: unity, or at-one-ment. The only thing necessary is becoming one with God, or Christ, and in perfect harmony with the spiritual universe in which we live. We have not to create harmony or perfection – we have only to come into tune with the divine harmony which forever *is*.

As soon as we come into tune with the divine harmony, everything falls naturally into its right place. Therefore, instead of begging and beseeching God to heal us, we should sit quietly in the Silence – which is the Presence of the Divine – and allow the Spirit to melt away all conflict, repression and complexes, all resentment, envy and selfishness, and to drive away all fear. Then can we become so merged into the Divine, and so at one with the heavenly vibrations, that the Life and Health of God can find expression in us.

I am not a doctor, and therefore do not lay claim to any medical knowledge, but a wide experience with the troubles of thousands of people confirms me in the belief that the root cause of disease and ill health is mainly conflict, disharmony, wrong feelings and emotions – worry, fear, anxiety, strain, and other forms of what we call 'wrong thinking'. Now, all these destructive things melt away when we come into tune with the divine harmony – when we cease resisting and learn to relax instead.

Resting in the Truth – or in the Lord, as people used to say – is the great secret. *Rest*! How many of us know what this really means? Let us all cultivate it.

> I rest in the Truth and come into tune with the
> Divine Harmony.

Because God's life is flowing into us, every change that takes place in our body is a change for the better. There may be upsets or disturbances at first – but these are due to the higher vibrations breaking down morbid accumulations, thus making ready for the finer life that is to follow.

> The larger and richer life of God now flows through all my being, making me perfectly whole.

Because we put our trust in God, and because God can express only perfection, every change must be for the better – so that year by year a more stable and normal state of health is attained.

There is, indeed, a larger and richer life than the ordinary life of the body. This greater life flows into us if we make contact with it and open ourselves to it. This diviner life not only invigorates – it also heals, restores, comforts and rests. It drives out all morbidness from the body; it removes all tendency to disease; it makes every day a better day for our health and well-being.

The knowledge that this richer life is flowing into us enables us to rest and have no care for the morrow. It does not matter what is wrong with us – the larger life produces perfection in its place. We do not have to concentrate upon this trouble or that, but only to contemplate God, allowing His rich, invigorating, healing, renewing, strengthening, purifying life force to flow into us, possessing us and making us anew, more after the Divine Likeness.

> Truth is wholeness. Wholeness is perfection in every part, in every direction, and to an infinite degree.

> This wholeness is inherent in each one of us: it is a jewel covered and hidden by the rubbish of error. All that we have to do is to eliminate the error so that the true wholeness can be revealed. This we do by believing in wholeness as the Reality of God; by declaring the truth of God's Wholeness, and by letting Truth demonstrate Divine Wholeness in our bodies. We have to do nothing ourselves, as regards healing, but simply to declare the Truth, persist in such declaration, and then see God do the work.
>
> The Way of Escape, H.T. Hamblin

Health is inherent. In spite of all the disorder on the surface, health or wholeness is the reality – the eternal truth, the Divine idea. God and His idea are one and perfect, and the only real. There is really nothing else. Everything else – such as disease, disorder, poverty – is not real; it has no life of its own, no substance – it is an absence of the real and true, a departure from the perfect Divine Order which is the only reality.

Health and wholeness form part of the Divine Order. Disease, sickness, ill health form no part of the Divine Order. There is only the Divine Order in reality. There is only one Creator and He, being perfect, can create only Divine Order and Perfection. Therefore, there is only the Divine Order, and the disorder of disease and sickness is not.

"How is this?" the beginner asks. The answer is that what we call evil is an absence of good. Good is the reality; evil is a privation or absence of that which is real – of that which is good. It is nothing in itself, not a new thing, only an absence of that which *is*.

All disorder in the world is said to be the result of sin. This is easy to understand when we realise that sin, in its original meaning, is a falling short. "We all have sinned and come short," said St. Paul. This puts the case in a nutshell. It is because we have fallen short, in consciousness, of the Divine Ideal concerning each one of us that we are as, and what, we are.

This is the reason why health is so intimately related to, and intermixed with, conduct, thinking and feeling. Wrong conduct, wrong thinking, and wrong feeling produce disease and misery indescribable – as a visit to our hospitals and asylums will show, if we need any proof. What is not so evident is that right action, right thinking, and right feeling produce the opposite condition of health and happiness.

Merely to refrain from various forms of evil thinking is only the first step in the way of Truth. The thinking must be positive and constructive. The thoughts must spring from the central idea of health, wholeness and harmony.

The statements we use should embody the truth that God is health and wholeness, and that we, as divine children, share with God this perfection. Because God is health and wholeness, and is the only reality, nothing but health and wholeness can come to us, or be expressed by us. As children of God, we share with the Divine His Infinite Life, Health, Wholeness and Power.

> Because Thou art Infinite Health and Wholeness, and art the only reality, I can express nothing but Thy Life, Perfection and Power.

When faced by suggestions, thoughts or feelings of sickness and the fear that these produce, what is needed is a quick reversal of thought; and there is nothing more effective than a rapidly uttered statement of truth such as "God is my health". What the actual words are does not matter, so long as they acknowledge God as the Source of all Life and Wholeness and affirm our oneness with the Divine as children of the One Source. This is the Truth, and Truth always kills error. We have not to contend with symptoms. All that we need to do is to affirm and declare the Truth in the face of all that is contrary to it. Truth then manifests itself just as the truth of mathematics becomes manifest as soon as its rules are followed. This teaching must be put into practice if its effectiveness is to be experienced.

A certain ill health or passing illness may be, at times, due to spiritual causes. At some stages of unfoldment and regeneration, changes take place in the body such as no physician can understand. At such times, it is necessary to slacken or suspend one's activities until one is strong enough to proceed. While keeping in this quiet state, a very light yet nourishing diet should be followed, and the mind quietly stayed upon God. Those who feel oppressed as though a weight were laid on their chest, and who consequently experience a difficulty in breathing, should not be alarmed. It may merely be a temporary inconvenience due to the natural development of an inward spiritual breathing. However, this does not concern the majority of people.

Another cause of ill health is emotional. It is extremely harmful to allow one's emotions to be aroused without finding a due channel of release. We can use the emotional energy that has been aroused in doing some kind of action or service to someone who needs it, or in some useful work. All emotions should be made use of in some way – the lower being transmuted into the higher.

We can never find health by thinking and speaking of, or directing our attention to, ill health.

It is useless to concentrate upon symptoms, or certain forms of ill health or disease; but if we turn our attention to that which is inherently whole, directing our mind to that which is perfect instead of upon that which is imperfect, we cannot fail to manifest an ever–increasing measure of wholeness, health and physical well–being.

For health is inherent. It is the natural state for humanity, just as perfection is inherent in the universe and is the only reality. It manifests naturally in so–called primitive people, and also in some types of mentally disturbed individuals where the subconscious seems to take control. In advanced, highly civilised and sensitive types, however, it often refuses to manifest until there is established a perfect balance between spirit, mind and body. There has to be spiritual health, moral health, mental health, and obedience to physical laws before the inherent health can find expression.

All this may sound rather complicated, but it is not so really, for everything falls into its proper place if we seek oneness or at–one–ment with the ONE – our Divine Source. Every form of disharmony in life is due to the fact that, in consciousness (but not in reality), we are separate from God. Therefore, by seeking oneness or union with our Divine Centre, we are travelling the only Royal Road to deliverance from all our troubles. It was because of this that our Lord said: "Seek ye first the Kingdom of God and His righteousness, and all these things shall be added unto you".

> Looking to Thee, I am filled with renewed life and power.

People sometimes say that thought control is no good – at any rate, in their particular case. They have tried it, and they are none the better. But it is easy to see why such people are no better. In spite of what they say, it is obvious that they have never changed their habit of thought at all. Their thinking, both conscious and unconscious, is still conducted from the standpoint of separateness. They also think from the standpoint that the visible is the real – whereas, of course, it is nothing of the kind. Things are not, really, as they appear to be. We are not separate from God and from one another.

It is because we believe ourselves to be separate, and think from this standpoint of error, that our life is filled with disorder and disharmony. The visible is not the real, and the tale that our senses tell is not a true one.

What, then, is right thinking? It is not only thinking thoughts of purity, love, goodness, beauty, charity, meekness, and in harmony with the Will of the Highest – it is also, and in addition, thinking from the standpoint of the eternal truth of our true relationship to God, which carries with it the inherent perfection of the Spirit. "Beloved, now are we the children of God", and in this truth we discover ourselves to be every whit whole.

> I open myself to the inflow of God's eternal Life and power and am made perfectly whole.

Chapter Fourteen

Prayer

There are so many varieties and degrees of prayer – from crude appeals to the unseen powers for the gratification of ambition or appetite, to the rapture of the saint who cries: 'God, of Thy goodness, give me Thyself, for only in Thee have I all' – that at first sight it is difficult to find much in common between them, or to arrive at any satisfactory definition of prayer. Some prayers are not even moral, some of the highest do not contain any petition at all, yet all are recognised as expressions of a common human instinct.

A closer study, however, shows that prayer, like everything else in the universe, is subject to the law of evolution. Each type is more especially suited to a particular stage of development, and depends for its success upon its reasonable correspondence not only with the actual conditions – physical, emotional, or mental – of the outer world, but with the habitual interests and attitude of mind of the petitioner, while prayers which are useful at one stage may be positively harmful at another, and some kinds of prayer cannot be employed at all by any except highly developed people.

W. Wybergh, The Shrine of Wisdom

From the above, it will be seen that prayer is not the same to all people. But before we can profitably discuss the subject, we must first state what prayer is not – or what, in its nature, is a malpractice and is not prayer at all.

Prayer is not sending commands down to the subconscious.

Some time ago, we had the doubtful pleasure of reading a series of articles on how to force the subconscious mind to give us all that we want. In one sense, the author made the subconscious her god – but she did not worship her god. She made it her slave, or that was her intention. Each day, she made a practice of putting aside half an hour or so, when, in the privacy of her bedroom, she would exercise all her willpower in commanding the subconscious mind to bring her what she wanted – a satisfactory letter from her house agent telling her that her flat was let at a good rental to good tenants – that a certain opening she very much desired should become hers, and so on. This was her substitute for prayer. But it was not prayer. It belongs to the category of black magic. Not knowing anything about incantations and the formulae of black magic, this poor deluded one could not do very much harm – but she had taken the left-hand path, which leads ever downwards.

> Making use of metaphysical treatments in order to compel our life to be what we think it ought to be is not true prayer.

With many, unfortunately, metaphysical treatments are merely a method of tinkering with results. Some disharmony appears, and immediately they set to work to remove it. When this has been wiped out, other disharmonies take its place. And so on, *ad infinitum*. The reason why this method of meeting life's experiences is wrong is because it takes for granted that life's experiences are evil, whereas they are essentially good. There is nothing evil in life's experiences. Those with a measure of spiritual insight know that we attract to ourselves just those experiences which are necessary for our unfoldment. When these experiences are taken in the right way and made a subject of true prayer, the result is great blessing and benefit. We each have lessons to learn in this life, and we can learn them, gain wisdom, and make progress in our unfoldment only to the extent that we co-operate with life and its experiences instead of opposing them.

In order to prevent any misunderstanding, we must point out that we do not suggest that life's troubles should be given into. Far from it – but what we do suggest is that they be overcome in a fundamental way. That is, by removing the cause. Metaphysical treatments aimed merely at removing effects can achieve no permanent results, but rather increase the disorder of life. It is like a person suffering from headache using headache powders. The headache is a symptom – and a serious one, often – of inward physical disorder. To use headache powders or other drugs is suicidal, for it increases the trouble ultimately, while all the time the inward disorder, which is the cause of the headache, is untouched. A wise person, therefore, would not use powders but would seek the cause of the headaches and remove it. Then the headaches would cease.

In the same way, the disorders of life can be overcome only by removing the cause. This cause is a lack of harmony within. There is a lack of adjustment with the true spiritual world or plane of perfect ideations. The higher mind and will are not at one with the Christ mind.

But a prayer is a turning to God. In the methods described, the one who makes use of them usurps God's place – or tries to. They want to dominate the situation. They acknowledge no divine guidance, but want to alter life according to their own ideas of what it ought to be.

Prayer acknowledges God as the Supreme Being. Therefore, our Lord taught us to begin by saying: "Our Father which art in heaven, hallowed be thy name."

Prayer, then, is the turning to a higher Being – the Supreme Being; to a higher power – the One Omnipotent Power behind all things. We acknowledge divine greatness and our dependence upon it.

The other kind of mental work that we have described is not prayer, but is of the same nature as magic. Prayer saves the soul through bringing it, ultimately, into union with God; magic, on the contrary, casts the soul into outer darkness.

While all prayer is a turning to God – or to an unseen Power greater by far than humanity – there is a vast difference between the prayer of the beginner and that of an advanced soul; and there are many grades in between. The prayer of the former is a crude appeal for help – either for deliverance out of trouble, or for the satisfaction of some ambition. The prayer of the most advanced worker in the Divine Art is a contemplation of God. As someone has said of the latter: the soul becomes poised like a bird on outstretched wings, contemplating with ineffable joy and bliss the Infinite and Eternal. It is possible for the advanced worker at any time, in a moment, to raise consciousness to a plane that transcends even thought, and to make contact with the Divine. Then it seems as though the floodgates of the river of life were opened and allowed to flow into the soul; then it seems as though all the songs of the redeemed were bursting the heart; then it seems that bliss ineffable so possesses the soul that nothing more is needed. God has given the self – and that is sufficient.

But there are many steps to climb before this wordless, thought–transcending stage of contemplation is reached. From petitionary prayer upwards is a long journey; but while it may be true, as stated by some, that one may possess greater ability than another, the principal thing necessary is practice. Practice makes perfect, and if a seeker after Divine Union will set aside part of each day to prayer and communion with God, they cannot fail to make steady progress.

All true prayer is a returning to God transcendent – to a Power and Wisdom far greater than ourselves. The lowest grade is petitionary: we beg and beseech God to bless us, to remove certain things from our life, to help us, or to give us particular things. Later, when we become more advanced and experienced in prayer, we may smile at such petitions, because we know that God withholds nothing – that God loves always, blesses always, helps always. But though we may smile at our former prayers, we yet realise that they were necessary. Prayer of this type belongs to a certain stage of spiritual development. It is helpful and acceptable to the beginner, to whom the more advanced forms would be useless – and perhaps even harmful. Therefore, the masses are always taught petitionary prayer.

Those, however, who are more advanced realise that their prayers are already answered, and that God withholds nothing, but simply gives the Divine Self – all that is, and all that can be. Prayer to them becomes a series of thanksgivings for all the blessings of life. The student of Truth praises God because all things are already bestowed, and all that is necessary is that they be expressed or brought into manifestation. This form of prayer is very much more advanced than the petitionary type, and it may take years of persevering practice to attain it.

Thus, the masses are rightly taught to say: "Lord, have mercy upon us. Christ, have mercy upon us." But the one who is more advanced in the art of prayer will bow the head in deep thankfulness, giving thanks from the depths of the heart for the wonderful mercy of God, which forever is, and which is never withheld. As they meditate on the mercy and love of God – which have followed them all their days – they are humbled to the very dust, yet filled with indescribable joy. This humility is always the sign by which those who are in the true path may be recognised. It comes through realising how great is the mercy of God.

At the beginning of the path, we are still attached to the world and personalities, and blinded by sense, such that we desire of God certain things. We may be in difficulty, but instead of begging God to deliver us, we quickly realise that God is doing the best thing for us in the circumstances – that Infinite Love and Wisdom have our case in hand, and that our trouble is only the necessary preparation for entrance into, or manifestation of, something far better.

The first stage of prayer might be illustrated by the Psalmist's words: "Then cried I unto the Lord, and He delivered me out of all my trouble." In the second stage of prayer, the one in trouble would turn to the Lord, and by coming into complete harmony with the Divine Mind, realise that the Lord was working on their behalf – and that all the trouble was due to Love and Wisdom adjusting matters and bringing about a better state of affairs, in spite of human mistakes and sins.

Actually, of course, the trouble is caused by human disorder. If humanity did not depart from the true path, there would be no suffering or trouble when Divine Order manifested itself. But this is a deep subject, and these are simple lessons, so we will move on now.

Then there is the third stage of prayer – meditation. This is the royal road to attainment. By meditating quietly upon God, we become changed, for the effect of meditation is to change us into the likeness of that upon which we meditate. One who meditates upon God becomes godlike. A further stage is contemplation. The soul then rises and remains poised above the earthly plane and contemplates the Divine. This is accompanied by a sense of beautiful mystic light. Such experiences are too sacred for words and too great to be described.

Each kind of prayer has its uses and is suited to the needs of the individual at the time. All types of real prayer are of the utmost value – not in altering circumstances, but in bringing the soul into union with the Divine. When this takes place, the Kingdom is found, and all things are added. Whenever we turn to God, we open ourselves Godward, with the result that the power of the Divine Life flows into us, transforming us and making us anew in the Divine Image. Through regular prayer or meditation, our spiritual life grows and flourishes amazingly; but if we neglect this daily communion with God, our spiritual life dies a natural death.

In the wonderful providence of God, it is planned that the lower should be raised to the higher – that the material should be transmuted into the spiritual. It is because humanity does not, or will not, recognise this that most of the trouble in life arises. We are out of harmony with the motif of life. We want to be happy and comfortable on this lower plane, instead of becoming changed and fitted for a higher one. We want to keep to a low vibration, but heaven is calling us to a higher – therefore there is conflict and suffering. Even professing Christian people are like this. They complain that as soon as they get comfortable, some trouble comes and upsets everything, and that no sooner is one trouble overcome than another appears. This is because they are not cooperating with the principle of transmutation – of raising the lower to the higher. When we recognise this principle or law of change, and think, speak, act and live accordingly, not only do things go more smoothly, but we also make great progress in our spiritual life.

The greatest help is that of prayer. Prayer should not be a request for the discipline of life to be removed, but for greater strength, wisdom and steadfastness with which to meet and overcome life's difficulties. It does not follow, however, that any request need be made. As we have already said, the highest form of prayer contains no requests at all, but is purely contemplation. Yet all forms of prayer are the same in one respect, which is that they are a returning to God – an acknowledging of a power and wisdom greater than our own. This affirms the sovereignty of God and expresses a desire that God should do for us that which we cannot accomplish ourselves.

Thus, though the beginner may want this or that done, and beg and pray for God to do what they think ought to be done, yet, in a deeper sense, there is also a desire that God's will should be done. Therefore, even the crudest of prayers is beneficial.

Every time we turn to God, desiring that the Divine should undertake for us, we are blessed, for we open ourselves to Christ's regenerative life. One whose prayer is simply contemplation opens themselves most to the Divine life and power, while one who asks for specific things opens themselves least – but all are opened to the sweet, vivifying, transmuting influences of the Spirit.

CHAPTER FIFTEEN

Blessing and Forgiveness

Each method of prayer is useful. One form is helpful to one, but useless to another, and vice versa. Each person should use the form of prayer that seems easiest and most natural to them.

Those who still feel that they must ask for things can put their prayers into more positive language. Instead of saying, "We beseech thee to hear us, good Lord", they can say, "We thank Thee, Lord of heaven and earth, because Thou dost always hear us, and that Thine ear is always open to our cry". In place of the appeal, "Lord, have mercy upon us", they can say, "The mercy of the Lord is from everlasting to everlasting upon them that fear (meaning, we think, honour, respect, obey, recognise the sovereignty of) Him, and His righteousness unto children's children; to such as keep His covenant, and to those that remember His commandments to do them".

It is useless to keep on repeating, "Lord, have mercy upon us", if the one who prays has not had mercy upon their fellows. If mercy has not been extended to those who have caused harm, how can any of us find mercy in God? It is utterly impossible. God's mercy is just the same – it is never withheld in the slightest degree – but we cannot enter into it until we have shown mercy to all people.

In the same way, it is useless to keep praying that God should forgive us our sins, or trespasses, or debts, if we have not forgiven others their transgressions against us. "For if ye forgive men their trespasses, your heavenly Father will also forgive you: but if ye forgive not men their trespasses, neither will your Father forgive your trespasses." How foolish, then, to keep on begging and praying God to forgive us if, at the same time, we harbour unforgiveness towards others.

> Therefore, if thou bring thy gift to the altar, and there rememberest that thy brother hath ought against thee; leave there thy gift before the altar and go thy way; first be reconciled to thy brother, and then come and offer thy gift.
>
> Matthew 5:23-24 KJV

It is not that God does not forgive, but that by our lack of forgiveness toward our neighbour we keep ourselves out of God's forgiveness and mercy. The remedy is plain: to forgive completely, have mercy upon all, and live righteously. Then all the blessings of God become ours. But no amount of supplication can accomplish this otherwise – even though it may be couched in correct psychological language.

It will be seen, then, that one who supplicates can never derive any benefit from prayer if they have not forgiven others, become reconciled to their fellows, and shown mercy in all their dealings. We must modify this statement to this extent – that the one who prays must at least desire to forgive or extend mercy. They may be so influenced by old habits and wrong upbringing that, although they desire to love all people and forgive and show mercy, they feel unable to do so. If, then, they breathe a prayer to High Heaven for help in forgiving, then be assured that this prayer is both heard and answered.

We cannot enter the Secret Place of the Most High until all our animosities and dislikes have been cast out. Until we forgive others, our prayers are merely a beating of the air. We must remember that God is no respecter of persons. God loves our enemies and those we dislike just as much as He loves us – no more, no less. The idea that we can curry favour with God at the expense of someone else must be replaced by the recognition of the universal parenthood of God, and the brotherhood and sisterhood of all people.

We cannot approach God, nor can we enter into any intimate communion with the Divine, until we hold all people in thoughts of goodwill – even those who seem to us objectionable or dangerous. We rightly hate the crime, but we hold the person in thoughts of goodwill. When we have dropped all thoughts of animosity, resentment and dislike, then we can enter into the Inner Presence – but not before.

It is a great help to prepare ourselves for prayer by sending out blessings to all people – especially those who have wronged us, those we dislike, and all who have aroused in us any feeling of resentment. By blessing them and sending thoughts of goodwill and benediction – by desiring for them and declaring for them all the blessings we ourselves enjoy, especially knowledge of the Truth – we prepare ourselves for intimate communion with the Most High.

We must remember this: that even one lingering resentment, one corner of the heart kept back from God and His searching light of truth, is enough to keep us out of the Kingdom of Heaven.

But the blessing we send must be real, sincere and genuine. We cannot deceive God. It is useless to pretend to forgive and bless, merely to approach God. We may deceive ourselves, but that is all. However, if our forgiveness is real – if we genuinely bless those whom we have disliked or resented – then not only are we ourselves forgiven, but our love and forgiveness become an open sesame to inner and intimate communion with the Father of all spirits.

The spiritual life is one of surrender. First one thing, and then another, has to go. But we are only ever called to surrender what is hurtful to us. We are asked only to give up what keeps us from our highest joy. When we have given these things up, we see that they were not worth keeping – that they were worthless in themselves, and that, in addition, they kept us completely out of the richer and fuller life of the Spirit, which is filled with joys and delights indescribable. All that we give up in our quest for God is worthless – all that we gain is precious beyond rubies and fades not away.

Man's idea of prayer is to ask or beg God to give them something, or to do them some favour. They want to receive but do not wish to give anything up. They desire to retain as much as possible, and yet to have things added. But the way of the Spirit is quite different from this. Our Lord taught that the path to attainment is by surrender. We have to give up our whole life, and ourselves, and all that we are or think we are, and all that we have or think we have. Then, when we have surrendered all and have given ourselves entirely to God, and become sufficiently humble, we find our feet in the narrow path that leads to the Kingdom of Heaven. Then we discover that we have given up the rubbish, receiving in its place the supreme treasure — a treasure so precious that there are no words to describe it.

But in addition to possessing heavenly treasure — the spiritual Kingdom — we find that all things are added in our external affairs: harmony, happiness, peace, supply, freedom from care, and everything that is essential to a truly perfect life.

"Seek ye first the Kingdom of Heaven and all these things shall be added unto you." We are therefore enjoined not to pray for things, or to ask God to do this or that, or to deliver us out of certain difficulties, for so we simply increase the disorder of life. All that we have to do is to seek the Kingdom of the Spirit. When once we enter the path which leads to the Kingdom and obey its rules, seeking only that God's will should be done, and that Divine

Wisdom should guide us entirely, then everything in our life tends to fall into its proper place, so that harmony and order begin to take the place of disharmony and disorder. Then we realise that if our special prayer for this thing or that had been answered, our trouble would have increased.

The true object of prayer, then, is to clear something out of the way that prevents our access to the Kingdom of the Spirit — the Kingdom of God or Heaven, of which our Lord forever speaks.

Many are the barriers which have to be broken down, but the principal one is the "bloated self". What we need most to realise in our prayer is that Christ is all, and we are nothing.

None of self, but all of Thee.

No approach can be made to God while the self stands in the way. When we think that we are something, or of any importance at all, we bolt and bar the door against ourselves. Worse is it when affirmations are used to this effect, declaring that we are IT.

A friend and teacher of the gospel of the Kingdom related the following incident. A man came to him and said that he had been receiving the instructions of another teacher, but that he was not getting on at all. In answer to the question "Why?" he said, "The affirmations given do not suit me." One of these, it appeared, was "I am God". Our friend then said, "I will give you a different affirmation which will help you more, if you will use it." The man did so, and after a few weeks returned, greatly benefited in every way, and moreover, making progress spiritually. The affirmation given to him was: "I am nothing."

When we get the bloated self out of the way, God can enter and make our lives anew. As we are freed from egoism, Christ the Lord from Heaven can make His abode in our hearts. But we must ever worship Him in reverence and adoration. At no time must we even think that we are that One, much less affirm it — for such is the way to insanity, and worse. It is the path of humility and self–effacement that leads finally to union with our Lord.

By making this surrender, realising that of ourselves we are nothing, and that Christ is all in all, prayer becomes an intimate communion with an ever–present God, instead of a sort of speech made to a Being afar off.

We are only the soul who one day will become wedded to the Bridegroom, the Lord from Heaven. We have to be prepared, purified, changed, and refined by the influence of the Holy Spirit, and by experiences, tests and initiations, until we become "as a bride adorned for her husband" – adorned by the grace and loving kindness of the Divine.

When we are quite ready – and not a moment before – the Divine Union will take place. But this is so far ahead, it need only be mentioned. It is too sacred for discussion. We must, however, attend to the preliminary steps, for upon these everything depends. If, instead of cultivating humility of heart and mind, the beginner "elevates the ego", they shut the door in their own face. It is therefore necessary that the right start be made. Otherwise, prayer – which is the greatest power for good – is perverted into a form of self-glorification and evil. Then it is prayer no longer.

The object of prayer is, of course, to find God, or that kingdom of the Spirit of which our Lord Jesus was always speaking. It is not in order to get something out of God that we pray, but that we may find Him, and become one with Him in consciousness. Our prayer, if it is "right", opens up the way from our side. It has already been opened up, on the divine side, by our Lord. We, by our surrender and by the cultivation of humbleness of heart and mind, remove the barriers which prevent us from entering the path which leads to the kingdom of God.

Therefore, in our prayer we surrender ourselves entirely to God and Christ; we desire only that God's will should be done in us and through us; we cultivate the spirit of humbleness and humility, without which it is impossible to make any advance at all.

Many readers may say at this point that this is too advanced for them. They are in trouble of some kind and want to be delivered. We sympathise with them, but must point out that the only way of deliverance is to seek first the kingdom of God, after which all their life lacks will be added. Some may say that they do not want anything added: what they desire is for evils to be taken away. To this we have to reply that all the 'evil' of life is a lack or poverty: it is an absence of divine good. Nothing has to be removed, really, except our own pride, stubbornness or egoism. All that is needed is that divine good should be added. When we seek first the kingdom of God, all that is wrong in our life becomes adjusted, all its many lacks become filled, all its discord becomes changed into the harmony of divine love.

The object of prayer is simply and solely the nourishment of the inner life and the bringing of the soul back to God. We cannot, of ourselves, bring ourselves back to God, but by prayer, aspiration, meditation and contemplation, the obstacles – which are purely on the human side – are one by one removed by the Spirit, until at last divine union becomes possible. But while, in one sense, we of ourselves can do nothing, yet the process of regeneration demands our wholehearted co-operation. Indeed, we can make no progress if we do not make it the sole object of life, surrendering ourselves and all, in order that we may find God.

We have to lose our life in order to find the real life. We have to lose the life of the personality, in order that we may enter into the larger life of God. We cannot inflate our life so as to include the greater life of God. Trying to do so would be equivalent to a gnat attempting to swallow a camel. If the "I am It" type of affirmations are used, the self or natural ego is inflated and prevents the soul, at the very outset, from entering the path of attainment. The entrance is very narrow, and until we become small enough – humble – we cannot pass through it. This is why all great teachers have laid such emphasis on humbleness. Our Lord tells us to take the lowest seat at the table and wait until we are called up higher.

"Blessed are the meek," He says, which means those who are the reverse of being self-assertive.

"I am" affirmations tend to produce a false centre. They make the one who uses them imagine that they are the centre of the universe. This, of course, is the very opposite of what is required. What is needed is that our small centre should be brought into alignment or harmony with the one centre of the whole. Therefore, the aspirant prays: "Thy will, not mine, be done." He magnifies his Lord and humbles himself. "He must increase," said John the Baptist, "but I must decrease." This is the whole secret of attainment. Christ must increase, but we must decrease. By glorifying and "magnifying" our Lord, the little self gradually disappears, until "Christ is all in all."

Chapter Sixteen

Steadfastness of Spirit

The great benefit that trouble confers on us is that it calls us to prayer and throws us back upon God. "Then I sought the Lord," says the Psalmist, "and He heard me, and delivered me from all my fears." If it were not for trouble, we are afraid that few of us would ever really pray – that is, pray with any real earnestness. Says Jacob Boehme, in *The Supersensual Life*, Dialogue One, speaking of the pilgrim on the path to Christhood: "God is his blessing in everything. And though sometimes it may seem as if God would not bless him, yet is this but for a trial to him, and for the attraction of the Divine Love, to the end he may more fervently pray to God and commit all his ways unto Him." This is perfectly true, as many of us know by experience. We always attract to ourselves those experiences that are best for us at the time – that is, the best from the point of view of our highest good and our spiritual growth and unfoldment. All the experiences of life should but make us pray the more. When we are in trouble, we naturally pray the most, so that the result is that we become richly blessed. The trouble would probably have been unnecessary if we had prayed as intensely, earnestly and fervently before it appeared.

What we are all prone to do is to become slack, spiritually, when life is free from trouble. When we have not a care in the world – when our affairs are prosperous, when our social and domestic life is smooth and harmonious – we are apt to be lulled to sleep, and if it were not for the chill wind of adversity, we should never awaken again. But the bleak blast of spiritual winter blows on our soul, and we awaken in time to realise our peril – to seek God again and again until we find Him as of yore.

If we prayed as fervently during periods of ease and prosperity as when in trouble, then times of stress would probably not be necessary. It is mainly because we fail to keep up with our unfoldment that trouble is attracted to us. It is our own fault.

We need never be afraid of adversity, for it always throws us back upon God, thus saving our spiritual life from extinction. It is times of ease that we need to fear, for they often prove to be the undoing of the soul. If, however, we pray as earnestly and fervently during easy times as in times of trouble, then the latter become unnecessary – unless we are spiritually too ambitious.

The devil, we are told, always welcomes plenty of philosophy and religion (of a sort) so long as the path of Christhood is not entered. In one sense, it is true that as soon as we enter the path, our troubles begin. In another sense, it is equally true that they are ended. They are ended as far as the disharmony due to wrong thinking, sin, wrongful action, and so on, is concerned. For instance, if one has been given to drinking, then the troubles produced by this vice – such as domestic unhappiness, lack of employment, etc. – become things of the past. If one has been of a quarrelsome, fighting disposition, upsetting all one's neighbours, the disharmony produced by this sort of conduct becomes as a tale that is told. By leaving off these evil ways, harmony is naturally restored. This applies in a hundred different ways of a more subtle nature which need not be enumerated here.

In another sense, however, our troubles begin when we enter the path, for we have to pass through various stages of change and preparation in order to become new creatures in Christ Jesus and meet for the kingdom of heaven. This entails the learning of certain very important lessons. Step by step we advance, being promoted to a higher class only when we have learnt thoroughly our present lessons. This process of change or regeneration is divinely ordained and proceeds methodically according to law. If we keep pace with our proper growth, unfoldment and change, all is well. If we lag behind, we attract just the trouble that will cause us to throw ourselves in utter abandon upon God, seeking His face and desiring only that He should undertake for us and guide us.

It seems almost impossible for us to pray fervently enough while times are easy. And very seldom do we pray as we ought. Partly for this reason, the lives of many godly and godlike people are full of trouble and crowned with sorrow. For sometimes, in spite of their best efforts, they appear to lag behind. But sometimes also it is due to spiritual ambition.

Most of us are of a slothful disposition, spiritually, so that as soon as things become a little easier, we slacken our efforts heavenward, and do not seek God so earnestly as we should. And, as a result, we attract to ourselves experiences that tend to wake us up, sending us back, once more, to prayer, more fully alive to our peril.

But there are those who are other than this, who are not slothful, but rather too energetic. They are also ambitious, spiritually. They aim so high, wishing to make such rapid progress, that they naturally draw down upon themselves very difficult experiences. They aspire to enter heaven, but apparently are dragged through hell instead. The reason is, of course, that by being too ambitious they bring upon themselves the tests of many initiations instead of only one. They are then liable either to fail or to become discouraged. They are inclined also to think that they have committed some great sin that has brought their troubles upon them.

Those who, through a too-great ambition, have brought a host of difficult experiences down upon themselves need not despair, for if they are steadfast, the Spirit will see them through safely. There is always strength available sufficient for our need, no matter how great it may be. They should cease being too ambitious, and live one day at a time, relying entirely on the Spirit to see them through their troubles and tests, and to guide their unfoldment. Their prayer should not be that they attain fully now, but that God should undertake for them and lead them day by day, thus gradually restoring harmony and peace.

When passing through dark experiences of the soul, it has been found helpful to pray as follows. First, to acknowledge and declare that God alone can deliver us; next, to pray that God should undertake for us, because we of ourselves can do nothing, and there is no one who can help us (save God); then, to praise or thank God because He is delivering us out of our troubles, or dark experience, and is bringing Divine Harmony into every department of our life. The latter part of the prayer raises us on the wings of faith to a realisation of the Truth. This, in turn, restores us to a state of poise, calmness and power; it gives to us rest and peace.

Beginners often say that they cannot pray extemporarily – they need a form of prayer or pattern which can be repeated or followed. Our Lord has given us such a pattern in what is called "the Lord's Prayer". Unfortunately, instead of this being used as a pattern and a guide in prayer, it is generally repeated quite rapidly as a sort of formula, following a number of prayers that are not at all like it in construction or character. Our Lord did not say that we were to gabble this prayer over at the end of a number of other prayers, but that we were to pray after the manner or pattern of the prayer that He gave as an example. "After this manner, therefore pray ye."

One who will but use the Lord's Prayer properly, instead of gabbling it, will find that it will meet their every need. It is a perfect pattern which, when followed, leads the soul to God.

The prayer consists of a number of phrases and sentences which, if meditated upon, open up inner depths of understanding. If one phrase or sentence be held prayerfully and reverently in the mind, so that the light of the Spirit of Truth can shine upon it, then its true meaning, wonder and significance become revealed to the soul. So rich is this prayer found to be that it seems as though eternity, even, can never reveal all its wonders, beauties and hidden meanings. Instead of gabbling it over parrot fashion, we find that we can linger over it indefinitely. We find that it is not a formula to be repeated, but a subject for meditation and a model upon which to base our prayers, which, if followed, leads us into the inner presence of God. Even if we cannot yet pray after the manner of this wonderful pattern, yet we can be helped and blessed by it, if we say it over very slowly, taking one phrase or sentence at a time, resting and thinking quietly over it for a little while, before passing to the next – at the same time trying to understand the wonderful significance of each statement.

In subsequent lessons, each phrase or sentence will be examined, so as to make it easier for readers to meditate.

CHAPTER SEVENTEEN

Our Father Who Art in Heaven

Our Father,
Who art in Heaven

Our Father. What a marvellous revelation of God and our relationship to Him is contained in these two simple words: *Our Father*! "And call no man your father upon the earth," said Jesus, "for one is your Father, which is in Heaven." No longer are we children of sin, corruption and death, but sons and daughters of God – joint heirs with Jesus Christ. "For it doth not yet appear what we shall be (the spiritual body is hidden to physical sight), but when He shall appear we shall be like Him."

This staggering and overwhelming teaching of God as our Father is hinted at in the Old Testament but is not revealed fully until our Lord proclaims it with such astonishing clearness, directness and simplicity. In Psalm 103:13, we read: "Like as a father pitieth his children, so the Lord pitieth them that fear Him." How we do indeed pity our children and loved ones as we see them seeking for satisfaction in that which satisfies not – stretching out eager hands for the painted, gilded baubles of life, which burst in their grasp, or plucking the bitter fruit in which is corruption and death. What yearning is in our hearts as we pray that they may be drawn by the Spirit to "Him whom to know is life eternal".

How we pity our children in their efforts to do something with their life that is worthwhile – their strivings and strugglings after something better, after higher and better things. Our hearts are filled with pity, the more so because we can do so little for them.

And God is like this – just the same, only to a greater degree. God pities us like a father, but to an infinite degree. We probably can reach the limit of our pity. We may reach a point where it is exhausted, and we can pity no more. It does not seem possible to us, perhaps, but such is most probably the case. But it is not so with God. His fatherly pity is without limit and without end. Oh, how wonderful are the love and mercy of God!

But the Psalmist makes a qualification – he imposes a condition. He says that God's pity is for those who fear the Lord – that is, those who love and serve God and who try to do His will. This does not mean that God does not pity those who are yet far from Him. "But God commendeth His love toward us, in that, while we were yet sinners, Christ died for us," says St Paul, and when we were in the wilderness, God's Spirit sought us out and found us. What it does mean is that until we turn to God and seek His face humbly and diligently, we make contact with what appears to be a wrath principle – or a God of anger, of cold, hard justice bereft of love and mercy. But "behind a frowning Providence, God hides a smiling face". If we approach God humbly, penitently, with a contrite heart, we find Him to be Infinite Mercy and Undying Love.

> "For Thou desirest not sacrifice; else would I give it: Thou delightest not in burnt offering. The sacrifices of God are a broken spirit – a broken and a contrite heart, O God, Thou wilt not despise."

God is Infinite Love and Mercy, is no respecter of persons, and is so universal in His love that "He maketh His sun to rise on the evil and on the good, and sendeth rain on the just and on the unjust." God therefore does not confine His pity to those who fear Him, for His love and compassion go out to all – but it is only those who turn to God who are able to appreciate it or become conscious recipients of it. So long as man ignores God, or works against Him, his life is out of joint. He finds darkness and wrath instead of light and love. A hardened offender, when brought before a human judge, finds him stern and just, hard and inflexible. But a little child at home may find the same judge to be a very lovable, tender and humane father.

When, however, man puts God first, acknowledges Him as Lord of his life, and recognises Him as his centre and the centre of the universe, he can win his way through the darkness and apparent wrath to the peace that passeth all understanding, in which he finds God to be all love and mercy, long-suffering and infinite kindness.

And so the Old Testament, although it dwells more on the wrath principle than on the love aspect, teaches us that God is really a Father of infinite love, compassion and mercy.

But it is in the New Testament that this teaching comes as a mighty revelation. Jesus tells His astonished disciples: "And call no man your father upon the earth, for one is your Father, which is in Heaven." No longer are we children of "wrath", but of light.

We said just now that it is by acknowledging God – putting Him in His rightful place as the centre of our life and of the universe – that we are brought into a right relation, so that we can win our way through the darkness and apparent wrath into the light and joy of the mercy, love and compassion of God. Yes, but it is a terribly rough and difficult journey, and this is why our Lord came to help us: "For the Son of Man is come to seek and to save that which was lost." Yes, we have all lost our way in the darkness, and of ourselves cannot find the path back to God. "All we like sheep have gone astray; we have turned, every one, to his own way; and the Lord hath laid on Him the iniquity of us all." So our Lord came – and forever comes – to open up the way, and to be Himself the Way, so that we may be led through the darkness and apparent wrath to our Father, who is infinite love and mercy.

And so our Lord teaches us to pray, not to a God of wrath and vengeance, but to a God of infinite love and compassion, who is our Father.

So let us sit or kneel quietly, rising in prayerful meditation above the fret and turmoil of life, to that great open place where the Light of lights forever shines – that realm of peace, where the soul is alone with God – enshrining in our thoughts those two words: "Our Father". And even as we do so, time and space drop away from us, so that we enter into the Eternal. Ages may come and go, nations rise and fall; even the "dappled earth" itself may pass away, yet still we remain, safe in the Eternal. The past, the present, the future – all become one. There is only the one glorious *now*.

God is not only our Father here on this limited plane of consciousness, but He is also in the Light Realms – or Heaven. God is not only immanent, He is also forever transcendent. Therefore, our Lord teaches us to say not only "Our Father", but "Our Father which art in Heaven".

At one time the immanence of God was ignored, and men worshipped a Being who was afar off. In recent years, many have gone to the other extreme and have ignored God transcendent in their joy at finding that God is immanent with us, speaking to us in a thousand ways.

But our Lord teaches us to look up to our Father who is in Heaven – to One who forever transcends all that we can think of Him, and all that we may discover about Him or in Him.

Prayer, then, as taught by our Lord, is an act of worship. We commence by claiming God as our Father, yet we acknowledge Him as transcendent – far above all that we can think, understand or imagine.

The first thing, then, that our Lord teaches us with regard to prayer is that our Father is not a God limited to this world or sense plane, but is the God of Heaven. This is really the basis of all real prayer – turning to God and His perfect real creation or ideal nature: "Our Father which art in Heaven." Every time that we turn to God in this way, even though we are dumb, we open ourselves to all the influences of Heaven. "All the Divine forces hasten to minister to us." Divine life and power flow into us – recreating us, regenerating us, and making us new creatures after the pattern of Jesus Christ.

All the time during which we look up to our Father in Heaven, we are receptive to divine influences. We are not only on the side of the angels, but the angels are even more on our side also. The Lord fights for us through His angels and ministering spirits – but only does so if we continue looking up. If we look down, we cut ourselves off from heavenly influences and open ourselves to forces of destruction. Therefore, our Lord teaches us to look up to "Our Father which art in Heaven".

Chapter Eighteen

Hallowed Be Thy Name

We have not only to address God as our Father, and to acknowledge that, though immanent through His Spirit, He is yet forever transcendent, but we must wholly acknowledge the holiness of the sacred Name. Our Lord taught us to pray to God as our Father, but He keeps us from the error of lack of reverence by the words, *"Hallowed be Thy Name"*. Although we are allowed to call God by the loving and familiar name of *Our Father*, yet there still remains the holy and ineffable name which is so sacred it cannot be uttered by us ordinary people.

The words we are considering are an expression of the deepest and most reverent worship. It is an acknowledgement of the transcendent, ineffable nature of God. Without such an acknowledgement and act of worship, we cannot approach God, no matter how hard we may pray. The way of approach to God in prayer is one of deep and profound reverence. The more we know of God the deeper our reverence becomes. The Pharisee who said *I, I, I* did not find God, but the poor tax-gatherer, who smote on his breast, crying

"God be merciful to me a sinner," went down to his house justified rather than the other.

Today, we are liable to be misled into claiming for ourselves equality with God. Some quote in justification of this claim the words, "Let this mind be in you which was also in Christ Jesus: who thought it not robbery to be equal with God." (Philippians 2:5–6). Yet the meaning of the passage is entirely different from that which is claimed by those who, to prove their own case, take a verse or two from the Bible, remove it from its context, and give to it an entirely different meaning from that originally intended. What they mean to infer is that man is equal with God. In fact, some go further, arrogantly affirming that they are God. They overlook the fact that man is not yet *man*.

The meaning that St Paul sought to convey is the very antithesis of that which we have just described. We have only to read the context of the two verses quoted in order to see this quite clearly. Here it is:

> "Let nothing be done through strife or vainglory; but in lowliness of mind let each esteem others better than themselves. Look not every man on his own things, but every man also on the things of others. Let this mind be in you, which was also in Christ Jesus: who, being in the form of God, thought it not robbery to be equal with God: but made himself of no reputation, and took upon him the form of a ser-

> vant, and was made in the likeness of men: and being found in fashion as a man, he humbled himself, and became obedient unto death, even the death of the cross. Wherefore God also hath highly exalted him and given him a name which is above every name: that at the name of Jesus every knee should bow, of things in heaven, and things in earth, and things under the earth; and that every tongue should confess that Jesus Christ is Lord, to the glory of God the Father."

The meaning of this passage is very clear, but it is brought out still more plainly in Dr Weymouth's version, which is as follows:

> "Let the very spirit which was in Christ Jesus be in you also. From the beginning He had the nature of God. Yet He did not regard equality with God as something at which He should grasp. Nay, He stripped Himself of His glory and took on Him the nature of a bondservant by becoming a man like other men. And being recognised as truly human, He humbled Himself and even stooped to die – yes, to die on a cross. It is in consequence of this that God has also so highly exalted Him, and has conferred on Him the name which is supreme above every other, in order that in the name of Jesus every knee should bow, of beings in Heaven, of those on the earth, and

of those in the underworld, and that every tongue should confess that Jesus Christ is Lord, to the glory of God the Father."

Again, if we turn to Ferrar Fenton's translation, we find the passage rendered thus:

"If then, there is any encouragement in Christ, if any consolation from love, if any community of spirit, if any tender feelings and pity, fill my joy full; so that you may agree in thought, possessing the same love, intending with united hearts the same object. Never in self-seeking nor through vainglory; but, on the contrary, with good feeling considering others in preference to yourselves, not each scheming for himself, but rather each for others. Think this with yourselves, what was in Christ Jesus? – Who existing in the beauty of God, considered not His Divine equality an incitement to greed; but forsook Himself, taking the form of a slave; arriving in human appearance; and being found apparently like a man, He humbled Himself, becoming subject to death – yes, a death of crucifixion! Therefore, God highly exalted Him, and freely gave Him the name surpassing every name; so that in presence of the name of Jesus every knee should bend, of celestials, and terrestrials, and subterrenes, and every tongue confess the Lord Jesus Christ exists in majesty of a Father God!"

The teaching of this passage overthrows once and for all the error of thinking that man is equal with God or is God. It gives the whole idea the lie direct. This passage teaches humility, reverence and self–sacrifice. These form the narrow gate through which man can alone obtain entrance to the Kingdom of Heaven. We recommend our readers to read and ponder over this passage – the second chapter of St Paul's Epistle to the Philippians.

And so, our Lord teaches us to be reverent and humble.

"Never in self–seeking, nor vainglory," but in humbleness of heart and true reverence to say:
Hallowed be Thy Name.

We can never be admitted into the intimate fellowship of the Secret Divine Innermost if we do not approach God in a spirit of deepest reverence, and in an attitude of worship and adoration. If we attempt to skip this stage – to leap exultantly over it – we do not find God, but only a cleverly disguised substitute, who does not truly reveal himself until, maybe, it is too late.

We can always distinguish between the true and the false mysticism. The true teaches the path of humility, self–abnegation, self–sacrifice and surrender. The false ministers to the self and to the unregenerate man's love of power, all spiritual achievement being for self's sake.

Like a surgeon's scalpel, the teaching of Christ severs and divides, cutting its way right through all false mysticism and philosophy. *What are you prepared to give up?* it says. *Are you willing to give up everything, even yourself, and to kneel in humility before the Lord your God?*

It is advisable for us to linger over this part of the model prayer given to us by our Lord, for that which follows can do us but little good if we do not first enter into the atmosphere which the first sentence generates.

This first part of the prayer, if dwelt upon, brings us into a perfect attitude of worship. Saying the words *Hallowed be Thy Name* not only elevates God to His rightful position, it also brings Him near, so that with reverent hearts we can speak to Him as *Our Father*.

It seems that people can become too presumptuous in prayer and may forget how holy is the Sacred Name. No less a man of God than Isaiah cried out in anguish:

> "Woe is me! For I am undone; because I am a man of unclean lips, and I dwell in the midst of a people of unclean lips: for mine eyes have seen the King, the Lord of Hosts."
>
> Isaiah 6:5

Moses, another great man of God, was commanded to take his shoes from off his feet, because he stood upon holy ground.

It may be argued that the New Testament teaches a new order of things: that in it, God is revealed to us as a God of love, mercy and forgiveness, and Christ as our elder brother, the Son of God, the firstborn of many brethren. Yes, but we must not forget, for one moment, the reverence due to the Sacred Name, which may not be pronounced, but which can be adored.

So, by means of these four words, our Lord makes us give to God our reverence and adoration. There is so much in our heart, as we write this, that cannot find utterance. It is impossible to put into words more than a fraction of what we feel. We can draw nigh to God, as to a father – and what a most marvellous and wonderful thing this is – yet as we do so we must realise more and more how holy, and pure, and searching His Presence is. God with us, yet ever beyond us. Here the blinding Light, yet beyond this the Darkness that is the Light of Lights, which our spiritual retinae cannot register. Wonder upon wonder, joy beyond joy, bliss beyond bliss, ever ascending.

If we forget the holiness of the Sacred Name – if we attempt to approach without reverence and appreciation of the greatness and purity of God – we do not get very far. We only get as far as our lack of reverence will allow us to go. In effect, we pray to a lower deity, one who is no higher than our thoughts and ideas of God. In one sense, we create our own God; therefore, if we have no reverence for our God, then our God is no higher than ourselves. It is only by worshipping and adoring a God infinitely higher than ourselves that we can be raised to higher and better things.

To sum up: by using the words *Hallowed be Thy Name*, we ascribe to God all glory, honour, power, infinite goodness, and love, and every other perfection. Thus, the teaching of Jesus is in sharp conflict with the insanity of modern times, which arrogates to the self – the personal "I am" – all the perfections of the Divine Character.

Chapter Nineteen

Thy Kingdom Come

Thy Kingdom Come. We cannot utter these words without surrendering ourselves to God.

To me, it seems that it first means *let Thy Kingdom come* (Weymouth's translation gives this). Let Thy Kingdom of love and divine order – of righteousness and truth, of purity and sincerity – come into my heart and life, O Lord. Let it break down the old order of sin and selfishness, hate and animosity, impurity and lust, untruthfulness and insincerity, and reign supreme and unchallenged in the inner chamber of my soul – bringing all my thoughts, desires, appetites, and longings into captivity to Christ, the perfect flower of humanity, archetype of the human race, and saviour of all people.

We are only too willing to pray for God's Kingdom to come on the earth, but we are not as ready to let God's Kingdom be established in our own heart and life – aye, and body too. Yet this is what the prayer means, so it seems to the writer. God's Kingdom of love, purity, truth and sincerity cannot be established on the earth until it has first been allowed full sway in our heart. First within – and then without.

If our Lord were to establish His Kingdom all at once, before our heart had accepted Him and surrendered entirely to Him, the results would be most terrible for us. We would run hither and thither, calling upon the rocks and hills to cover us.

Spiritually speaking, when the earth is spoken of, it can be applied to ourselves – that is, the lower, unregenerate nature, or our wayward hearts. When we pray *Let Thy Kingdom come*, it is useless for us to think of it as some exterior event in which the Lord will make everything nice and easy for us, and very hot for the wicked people who live next door. What we have to realise is that it is in our own heart that God's Kingdom must be established – and this can be accomplished only to the extent that we surrender utterly and completely to the Divine Will.

> "Behold, I stand at the door and knock: if any hear my voice, and open the door, I will come in to them, and will sup with them, and they with me."
> Revelation 3:20

How the heart thrills at these words. They remind us of some lesser words, which likewise carry the same message in simple language – words which every surrendered heart must rejoice in, no matter how simple, uneducated, or – from the outer standpoint – ignorant one may be.

> *"Come into my heart, Lord Jesus,*
> *There is room in my heart for Thee."*

Not great verse perhaps – yet it breathes the right spirit of surrender.

Is there any room in our heart for the Kingdom of Heaven? We should not be too sure about it. We may go on for years thinking that we have the Kingdom within us – but something happens which proves to us that it is all self within, and not the Lord at all. We make what we believe to be a complete surrender to God, and yet later on we find that there is far more to be surrendered than ever we believed possible.

The text *"the Kingdom of Heaven is within you"* must not be taken too literally. Dr Weymouth suggests that it requires subjective, spiritual qualifications for its apprehension. He also offers *"is among you"* as an alternative rendering to *"is within you"*, meaning that it has already come into your midst, although as yet you do not recognise its existence.

The Kingdom of Heaven can be established in our heart and life only to the extent that we allow it to. We must surrender. We must open the door.

Therefore, we pray, in a spirit of full and complete surrender to God: **Let Thy Kingdom come.**

Not only is the prayer – *"Let thy Kingdom come"* – an expression of submission and surrender to the beautiful and joyful will of God, it is, so it seems to us, a prayer of invocation. *Let thy Kingdom come.* When we pray thus, in a spirit of invocation, it becomes a word of power that prepares the way of the Lord. It invokes omnipotence – it calls upon the Divine Order to manifest itself – it is as the voice of a prophet calling upon people to turn to God.

Used in this sense, the words become an expression of power. They call upon, and powerfully affect, the Divine Forces that are working invisibly to bring Divine Order upon the earth.

It is also a prayer of blessing and benediction. It calls upon High Heaven to establish on the earth the highest good of humanity. It calls upon the Supreme Lover to manifest upon the earth – to bring into actuality the Kingdom of Love and Goodwill in the hearts and lives of all people.

It is also a call to every soul – and to the one who prays – to help bring about a new social order, in which the principles of Christ's teaching are followed in business and public affairs, and in the treatment of those who are often termed 'the masses'.

> *"Bring me my bow of burning gold!*
> *Bring me my arrows of desire!*
> *Bring me my spear! O clouds unfold!*
> *Bring me my Chariot of Fire!*
> *I will not cease from mental fight,*

> *Nor shall my sword sleep in my hand,*
> *Till we have built Jerusalem*
> *In England's green and pleasant land."*

– William Blake

This prayer is not only a call upon Heaven – it is not only as the voice of a prophet calling people to God – it is not only a call to humanity to be active in all good works which have for their object the bringing of *Jerusalem* upon earth – it is also a dedication of oneself to the service of others.

Now, having in view all that these words mean, are we prepared to pray: **Let Thy Kingdom Come?**

Chapter Twenty

Thy Will Be Done

There can be no Heaven for any one of us until we *do* the will of God, instead of merely talking about it. The will of God is universal and ever-present harmony – or divine order. It manifests to the extent that we correspond to it. The difference between Heaven and hell is that the former is in harmony with the will of God, while the latter is at enmity with it. The will of God is a harmonious, beautiful and joyful movement, rhythm or vibration: we enter Heaven to the extent that we harmonise with it, conform to it, or vibrate in sympathy with it.

That this harmonising with the Divine Rhythm, or Vibration, or Will is the very basis of the New Life – without which no regeneration can take place – is plainly and emphatically stated by our Lord:

> "Not everyone that saith unto me, Lord, Lord, shall enter into the Kingdom of Heaven; but they that doeth the will of my Father which is in Heaven. Many will say to me in that day, Lord, Lord, have we not

> prophesied in thy name? And in thy name have cast out devils? And in thy name done many wonderful works? And then will I profess unto them, I never knew you: depart from me, ye that work iniquity."
>
> Matthew 7:21

Other passages might be quoted, but this is sufficient. We may be prophets, teachers, preachers, healers and doers of wonderful works – that is, we may take a leading part in the religious activities of our time and be looked up to by many – yet if our inner life is not in harmony with the Will of the Supreme, we are still outside the Kingdom of Heaven.

But the Kingdom of Heaven is open to those who can neither preach, teach, heal, nor do anything outwardly remarkable. It is open to all who live, think, act and love in correspondence with Heaven. It is only those who are completely at one with the will of God who become regenerated. Regeneration only proceeds when the will of the individual is in harmony with the Will of the Whole – the Supreme, or the Universal. Therefore, those whose will is not attuned to the Divine Will can never make progress towards finding the Kingdom of Heaven, simply because the transforming, regenerative process of inward change and renewal cannot take place. Nothing can happen until the will is at one with the Divine.

The Will of God – or Heaven, or the Father in Heaven – the rhythm of the Central Harmony of the real, inner, unsullied Universe which is the perfect expression of the Divine Idea, is a beautiful and lovely, joyful and joyous thing. It cannot be described. It is perfect harmony, peace, beauty, loveliness, music – and all that is delightful. All we have to do is to be *at-oned* with it, so that its vibration is our vibration, its rhythm our rhythm, its peace our peace. But it must not be thought that such peace is stagnation. It is rather the stillness of unimpeded activity.

There is only one way by which Heaven can be brought to earth – and that is by people acting, thinking and living as is done in Heaven. If everyone were to live, feel, act and think as is done in Heaven, then immediately earth would become Heaven. It would need no other change.

Such a change could take place only through Heavenly influences, but we can help in two ways. After all, it is the principal duty of every follower of Christ to endeavour – by their life and actions – to help extend the Kingdom of God upon earth, which simply means the bringing of Heaven upon earth.

Now, the two ways by which we can help to hasten the establishment of Heaven upon earth are these:

1. By praying the prayer given by our Lord – "Thy Kingdom come, Thy Will be done, in earth as it is in Heaven".

2. By ourselves living and acting as nearly as possible like those who live in Heaven.

An impossible task, you say? But we can all try; we can all do our best; we can all, at the very least, pray. We can all make a start – going forward with humility.

Let us begin with prayer. This is not a matter of telling God what to do, but is both an invocation and a surrender. When we use the words: "Let Thy Kingdom come, Thy will be done, in earth as it is in Heaven," we invoke the powers of Heaven to descend, purify our heart, and establish therein the Kingdom of Heaven. At the same time, by so praying, we make a surrender of our will to the Supreme Will. Our will then becomes aligned with that of Heaven, and the Divine Will becomes supreme on our earth.

Arising out of this, our life and actions become attuned to the Divine. We begin to practise a Heavenly attitude of thought, and in time, we become Heavenly–minded, so that, eventually, we grow into what Swedenborg calls a "Heavenly person". A Heavenly person is one who practises Heavenly ways – one who brings Heaven into all their actions and dealings with others, and who delights to do so, for nothing else gives such joy.

Thus we see how wonderful, fundamental and far–reaching is the teaching of our Lord.

CHAPTER TWENTY-ONE

Give Us This Day Our Daily Bread

O ur Lord does not teach us to ask for either riches or poverty. He never taught penury, but promised us that our needs would always be supplied if we place our trust in God, our Father in Heaven. In the book of Proverbs, chapter 30, verses 8 and 9, we read: "Give me neither poverty nor riches: feed me with food convenient for me." This is a very wise prayer and entirely in accordance with our Lord's teaching.

> "Give us our daily bread, Father – today, or day by day – just as manna was given to the children of Israel in the desert. We do not depend upon material sources but only upon Thee, for Thou art the one Source of our sustenance, as well as of our life. We can live only through Thee. It is Thy life that animates, it is Thy food that feeds us, it is Thy wisdom that guides us, it is Thy love that sustains and protects us. Thou knowest all our needs; do Thou, therefore,

> supply them, according to Thy will, out of Thy riches in glory by Christ Jesus. Take from us all that hinders the manifestation of Thy bounty. Remove from us all that keeps us from trusting entirely in Thee and Thine inexhaustible supplies. Give to us, Father, the faith which *knows* that Thou canst never fail us. Help us to realise that we possess in Thee an inner, secret, invisible source of supply that is infinite and which can never fail."

Our Lord wants us to trust the Spirit rather than the things that perish. He invites us to take our eyes from, it may be, visible lack, and to look with faith to the invisible and eternal.

The great point in all this is: *Do we believe that God is capable of feeding and sustaining us even though we might be on a desert rock in the midst of an ocean?* Do we believe that God's inner, invisible source of supply is ever open to us, no matter where we might be? Have we faith and vision enough to make contact with this inner, spiritual, creative ground of all things visible?

If not, then we have still much to learn. If we do not believe in miracles, then no miracles can ever "happen" in our experience. Such an attitude of mind naturally chains us to the material plane and to the harsh laws that govern business and social life. But if we think beyond these things – if we push back the boundaries of our mind and admit miracles into our scope of thought – then, and not until then, what we call the impossible becomes possible.

We must learn to think spiritually. We must think from the standpoint of what we truly know – the knowledge that we are spiritual beings, living in a spiritual universe, governed by spiritual law. It is only in this way that we can push out beyond the confines of time and sense and become liberated from the limitations of our present restricted consciousness.

All is now. There is really no such thing as anything "happening". Einstein's theory of relativity confirms the teaching of mystics and seers. *All abundance is, now.* It does not need to be created – it is here already, and always will be. All beauty is here now, could we but see it. All joy is here now, could we but enter into it.

It is only by prayer that our consciousness can be opened to receive this great truth. *Give us this day our daily portion.* We are taught to ask for nothing more – simply enough to meet the needs of the present moment. We may be overwhelmed by difficulty and apparent lack. We may dread the morrow with its financial responsibilities. But *"The Lord is my shepherd; I shall not want."*

If we trust the inner spiritual supply, it will prove to be sufficient for all our need. But we must trust, and we must pray—and we must take both very seriously.

Chapter Twenty-Two

Forgive Us Our Trespasses

> And forgive us our debts, as we also forgive our debtors.
>
> Matthew 6:12

The corresponding passage in *Luke 11:2* states: *"And forgive us our sins; for we also forgive everyone that is indebted to us."* Whether intentional or not, this phrasing surely offers encouragement to the soul. It says, in effect: *"If I, with all my frailty, can forgive those indebted to me, shall not the Lord of Perfection and Goodness forgive me?"*

We are often tempted to think of God as less forgiving than even a good person – but Jesus reveals a Heavenly Parent who forgives to the uttermost. The beloved St John tells us that God is love itself. Love, by its very nature, cannot withhold forgiveness. If we remain unforgiven, it is only because we have not stepped into the sphere of God's forgiving love. All we must do is meet the condition: to forgive those who have wronged us.

If we cannot forgive and love those who have caused us harm, how can we draw near to Infinite Love and Forgiveness? It is not possible, for we would be vibrating at a different frequency altogether. Love and forgiveness are of one vibration; bitterness and hardness of heart are of another. This is why we need a new heart – a heart of flesh instead of one of stone. It is God's love that softens us, transforming us into new beings, formed in the likeness of love.

> "Herein is love, not that we loved God, but that He loved us and sent His Son to be the propitiation for our sins. Beloved," says John, "if God so loved us, we ought also to love one another... We love Him because He first loved us. If a person says 'I love God' and hates their sibling, they are a liar. For the one who loves not their sibling whom they have seen, how can they love God whom they have not seen?"
> 1 John 4:10–11, 19–20 (adapted)

It is only the love of God – as revealed in Jesus Christ – that can draw us into the living circle of Divine Forgiveness. When we become aware of how far short we have fallen of the Divine Ideal, we may despair that God could forgive us. But there is no cause for fear. God has already forgiven us, for – as Paul proclaims – *"while we were yet sinners, Christ died for us."* (Romans v.8) Forgiveness is infinite, and the more humbled and unworthy we feel, the more ready we are to receive it or, rather, to enter into it.

Some suppose that Christianity asks little of its followers. Let such people try living it. To truly follow Christ demands more than many are prepared to give – and only a few persevere to the end. One of the hardest demands is to forgive completely: from the depths of our heart, without condition or reservation. It is not easy to let someone "get away with it." Yet it is in that very surrender that the gate to eternal life stands open – for there is no other way through.

The call to the Kingdom of the Spirit is a call to love, forgiveness, and self-surrender. If we are to enter it, we must follow Christ all the way. We are called to become Christs in miniature, following the path He has already walked for us. If we do this, allowing love to constrain and guide us, then:

> "the Spirit himself helpeth our infirmities, and maketh intercession for us with groanings which cannot be uttered."
>
> Romans 8:26

Yes, it is a great and weighty undertaking—to seek and find the Kingdom of God and eternal life. Yet even the simple and unlearned can walk this steep and narrow path, for it is not a matter of intellect, but of the heart. *"But the one who endures to the end shall be saved."*

"Him that overcometh will I make a pillar in the temple of my God, and he shall go no more out... and I will write upon him my new name."

Revelation 3:12

Chapter Twenty-Three

Lead Us Not Into Temptation

This part of the Lord's Prayer has always been difficult for most people. They cannot understand how a good God could lead His children into temptation – yet, if He does not, why are we taught to pray asking Him not to do so? On the other hand, some may reason that temptation is ultimately beneficial, for without it we could not grow or become wise and strong in character – and therefore, perhaps it is fitting that God should lead us into temptation, as a way of guiding us toward our highest ultimate good. But this line of thinking, of course, only makes confusion worse confounded – for if that were so, why would we be instructed to pray: "Lead us not into temptation"?

It is no surprise that these few words are considered to be among the most difficult and perplexing.

We do not believe there is any definitive intellectual explanation to this problem. The mind simply circles round and round – baffled at every turn. What the intellect cannot supply, however, may be revealed through experience.

Those who have wrestled with temptation in the spiritual life will likely agree that there are, broadly, two kinds of temptation. There are the spiritual trials inseparable from growth and deepening – such as our Lord experienced in the wilderness. Then there are the temptations we attract through our own lower nature – our unexamined desires, fears, wrong thinking, or indulgent thoughts. Christian, in Bunyan's immortal allegory, met Apollyon in the valley because his foot slipped on the way down the hill. Had his foot not slipped, he would not have encountered that trying and terrifying experience; for those who came after him – we are told – avoided Apollyon entirely, for their feet slipped not.

In the same way, temptation often comes to us because we have attracted it – through the harbouring of wrong thoughts. Even the smallest indulgence in unworthy thinking weakens our inner defences. This, in effect, is an invitation to the enemy – who waits until the walls are compromised, and then attacks. The real battle is not fought and lost at the moment of crisis, but beforehand – when we allowed that seemingly insignificant wrong thought to enter. If we had resisted the small temptation, the larger assault could never have broken through. The true battleground, then, is the thought preceding the act – not the act itself.

Therefore, we are taught to pray: "Lead us not into temptation" – meaning, lead us in such a way that we fall not into sin, and thus expose ourselves to the danger and trial of temptation. It is akin to praying that we may be kept from sin altogether – the deep desire of every earnest follower of God. It is a plea for protection from the small misstep that can open the door to a greater fall.

There is, however, another aspect – perhaps speculative, perhaps daring. Might it be that God can perfect us without temptation? Might it indeed be possible to remain so closely aligned to God – in prayer, in thought, in word and deed – that transformation comes as gently and naturally as the unfolding of a flower, without the need for trial or conflict? If this is so – and perhaps some living saint who has truly attained might bear witness – then the prayer "Lead us not into temptation" takes on a deeper, more radiant meaning. It becomes a prayer not only for preservation, but for the highest path – the path of grace, unmarred by needless struggle.

As to the passage "but deliver us from evil" – rendered in the Revised Version as "deliver us from the Evil one" – some translators, including Dr Weymouth, suggest "Rescue us from the Evil one" as the better reading, though he notes it may also rightly be rendered "from evil".

What is important is that we recognise the fact that there is an opposition, or enemy, always striving to drag us down into the mire again, in spite of all our efforts to climb to higher and better things. The more earnestly we seek Divine Union, the more subtle and persistent the opposition becomes. At times it seems as though our case is hopeless, so weak and helpless are we, and so clever and strong the enemy.

But when we awake to spiritual things and begin to live the spiritual life, we throw down the gauntlet to the enemy of souls. Yet so clever and powerful is our antagonist, we would be hopelessly defeated – and that most assuredly – if it were not for the Power greater than our own, upon which we can call.

All who seek Divine Union are subjected to the most violent assaults of the powers of darkness, till our prayer becomes a cry for deliverance from the Evil One. Then we do not hesitate to make use of the prayer given us by our Lord – yes, right lustily, and with complete abandon. And we find that we do not call in vain, for God both hears and answers prayer.

But when all frontal attacks have been beaten off, more subtle methods are employed. There is a lull in the combat; temptation ceases to all appearance, and the beginner thinks he has attained, and that temptation can never touch him again. But when he is quite off his guard, and resting in a false security, the tempter comes again – this time making no mistake. Down the aspirant falls, and in a most woeful way; and the last state seems worse than the first.

Now, the mistake which we all make at this stage is that we think too much of our fall and not enough of our Deliverer. To grieve or sorrow over our sin is good, in that it makes us humble and prevents us from ever being so foolish as to congratulate ourselves, thinking that we have attained, or, at any rate, have mastered the enemy. But to pay too much attention to our fall is a great hindrance. By directing the attention to our weakness, we increase and intensify it. Whereas, if we direct our attention to Christ, our propensity to sin dies a natural death through lack of attention.

It seems to us at this stage as though the forces of evil are not only bent upon our destruction, but that they must succeed – so strong are they, and so weak are we. But, if we refuse to pay too much attention to our failures and falls, keeping instead our eyes upon the Eternal Christ, the powers of darkness can succeed only in destroying "the old man" in us, thus making room for the new Christ–man who grows up in his place.

The old self or nature has to die, while in its place the new self or nature has to be born and grow daily until it reaches the full measure of the stature of Christ. The powers of darkness are not going to allow this to happen without a struggle, and this is why there is a Holy War continually waging during the process of re-generation. But there is a stage where rest takes the place of battle: "There remaineth therefore a rest to the people of God." There will come a time to those who are faithful when the enemy will depart forever, for there is **then** nothing in man over which he has dominion.

We said just now that the old self has to die. After starting to live the life of the Spirit, it is not long before we discover that the greatest "devil" that we have to fight is "self". We may sigh for the universal life and consciousness, but we must first give up our separate life – ourself, our "me" and our "mine". For a long, long time "self" continues to rear its head, demanding recognition – but it will surely die in time, if we refuse to give it attention, turning our attention instead to Christ. For a long time, it is I, I, I with us – which, of course, only increases our egoism and separateness. It is helpful to say, often: "Not I, but Christ." We can also say: "I am nothing, nothing: Thou art my Lord, my All in all."

Proceeding along the lines of humility and self-surrender, the old man of separateness dies, our spiritual nature swings to its true Centre, and we realise the Universal Consciousness.

More things are wrought by prayer
Than this world dreams of.
Wherefore, let thy voice
Rise like a fountain for me night and day.
For what are men better than sheep or goats
That nourish a blind life within the brain,
If, knowing God, they lift not hands of prayer
Both for themselves and those who call them friend?
For so the whole round earth is every way
Bound by gold chains about the feet of God.

Arthur Lord Tennyson

Also by Henry Thomas Hamblin

Thank you for purchasing this book. If you have enjoyed reading it, please consider leaving a review. It takes just a moment, and helps small publishers like us boost the visibility of our books, so that other readers can find our titles. You can scan the relevant QR code for your country of residence, by holding your phone's camera to the code. A prompt will appear, which will take you to the 'leave a review' page. Thank you – your time is much appreciated.

If you are in the UK, use this code	Scan with your phone camera
Scan the QR code or type this link into your browser **bit.ly/4nfcX7Y**	
Hamblin Vision Publishing	THANK YOU!

GOD'S LOVE, YOUR LIFE

If you are in the US, use this code

Scan the QR code or type this link into your browser

bit.ly/3GaoHI6

Scan with your phone camera

Hamblin Vision Publishing

THANK YOU!

If you are in Canada, use this code

Scan the QR code or type this link into your browser

bit.ly/465lUdN

Scan with your phone camera

Hamblin Vision Publishing

THANK YOU!

If you are in Australia, use this code

Scan the QR code or type this link into your browser

bit.ly/3TyZF8G

Scan with your phone camera

Hamblin Vision Publishing

THANK YOU!

Also by Henry Thomas Hamblin

The Stillness of the Infinite

18 Meditations to Deepen Spiritual Awareness through the Progressive Reflective Meditation Method

Thinking in Your Right Mind

Allow the Power of God to Change the Way You Think

Within You is the Power

The Inner Secret to Health, Happiness, Success and Abundance

The Secrets of Your Divine Powers

Reconnect with your Spiritual Self to Overcome Obstacles, Heal Your Life and Achieve True Success

The Spiritual Path to True Success

The Practical Mystic's Guide to Living Sucessfully

The Message of a Flower

The Divine Wisdom in Nature

The Worry Antidote

The Practical Mystic's Guide to Living Fearlessly

God the Source of Good

The Practical Mystic's Guide to Living Fearlessly

The Power of Thought

How to unlock the power of your mind to create a life of health, success and prosperity

Powerful Prayers and Psalm 23

The Practical Mystic's guide to three Christian Prayers: The Lord is My Shepherd, The Lord's Prayer and Bless the Lord, O My Soul

The titles below are available from our website www.thehamblinvision.org.uk

The Way of the Practical Mystic

My Search for Truth

The Story of my Life

Life Without Strain

Divine Adjustment

The Open Door

HENRY THOMAS HAMBLIN

Life of the Spirit

His Wisdom Guiding

The Hamblin Book of Daily Readings

God Our Centre and Source

God's Sustaining Grace

www.ingramcontent.com/pod-product-compliance
Lightning Source LLC
Chambersburg PA
CBHW030336010526
44119CB00047B/510